Once Upon a Cocktail acknowledges that the City of West Hollywood is sited on the ancestral and unceded homelands of the Gabrieleño Tongva and Gabrieleño Kizh (pronounced "Keesh") peoples, a land once known as Tovaangar (which includes hundreds of square miles of the Los Angeles Basin), and that is still home to many Gabrieleño Tongva. **We honor and pay respect to their elders and descendants—past, present, and emerging—we recognize and are grateful their vital stewardship of this land continues into our future.**

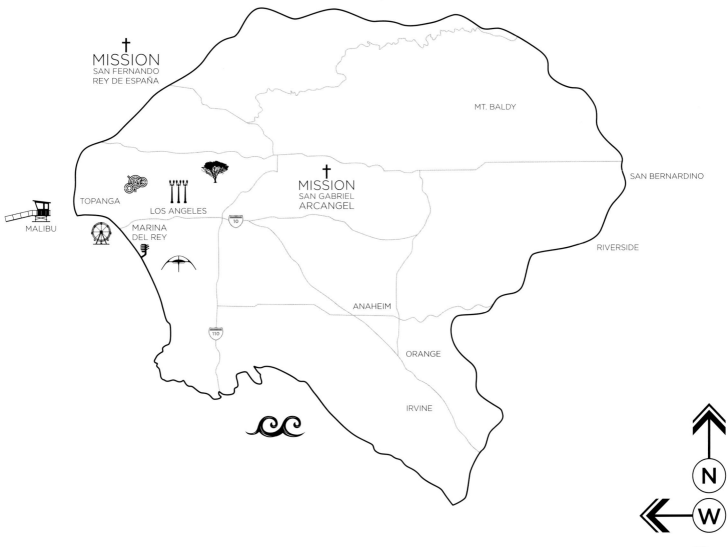

THIS BOOK IS DEDICATED TO DIVINE TIMING!

First Edition ISBN: 979-8-218-95985-2

Library of Congress Control Number: 2023913480

Lead author, all Illustrations, book cover design, & graphic design: Katie Brightside
Co-author & cocktail curation: Sarah L.M. Mengoni

Prepress and print management: Charles Allen, Sagest, Pasadena, CA
Final production files: Howard Morris, Sagest
Printed and bound in South Korea

The typeface Gotham* is licensed from Monotype.

In 1807, amongst an elite group of writers, New York City received the nickname Gotham.
The word derives from a medieval English word Gottam which literally means Goat Home.
The name caught on as a colloquialism, in the press and on buildings.

*The typeface Gotham is named after the urban landscape that inspired it, New York.
Designed by Jonathan Hoefler and Tobias Frere-Jones in 2000 for GQ Magazine.
The font was included in the MoMA permanent collection in 2011.

**The Brightside Fairytale font was created by Welcome to the Brightside™ in 2017 for the book
A Modern Moral, a series of original, commissioned artworks and revised fairytales.

onceuponacocktail.world

A cocktail recipe book featuring 54 of the most treasured
venues from across West Hollywood.

Once upon a Cocktail™

WEST HOLLYWOOD

BY
**KATIE BRIGHTSIDE
& SARAH L.M. MENGONI**

Welcome to the Brightside™

West Hollywood, California

Acknowledgments

Huge shout out to mummy bear for always listening, encouraging me to get back up, and go for it!

Thanks to Nick Rimedio for placing all the chips on the table and championing my extravagant ideas.

To Sarah L.M. Mengoni, for taking a trip of your life. You have been an asset professionally and personally—your talents and patience are beyond a thank you. Mark, I'm not sorry I stole your wife. I will steal her again, she's incredible, but cheers to you for cheerleading our passionate journey.

Nalani Santiago, you know what you did! Without your impeccable insight, knowledge, and friendship, I would be lost without you. To Erin Mohr, Linus and Gus, hopefully the extra work wasn't a huge disruption to the household.

RJ, is it too soon to make more blackberry salt?

I have much love for our co-producer, the West Hollywood Chamber of Commerce, spearheaded by our warrior, Genevieve Morrill. I am indebted to your passion for our city and standing strong to hold us all together. Gen, you and the team—Nalani, Jamie, John-Baptiste, and Alexa—are invaluable. I appreciate all that you do for me and The Creative City.

With much gratitude, I'd like to thank my emotional support team, Kirsty Ainsworth, Jessica Agapetus, Julian Tucker, Carolina Suero, Tina Karras and K. Ryan Henisey. You have all individually spurred my sanity and insanity with love, a pint, and never any judgment—it's just Katie being Katie. Ryan, Sir Master of English Literature, I will win Gin Rummy, watch me!

To all *Once Upon a Cocktail* partners and sponsors, Andaz West Hollywood, Barfly® Mixology Gear, Beam Suntory, Beverly High Rye, Caffè Borghetti, Botanist Gin, Branca USA, Casamigos, Chamberlain West Hollywood, City of West Hollywood, Cointreau, Dahlia Cristalino, Del Maguey, Dos Hombres, El Silencio, Fever-Tree, Hotel Ziggy, Kástra Elión, Ketel One, Kuleana Rum, Le Parc on Melrose, Liquid Alchemist, Montrose at Beverly Hills, Neft Vodka, Ophora Water, Q Mixers, Quechōl Sotol, Remy Cointreau, Scrappy's Bitters, The Sunset Strip BID, Tina's Vodka, Visit West Hollywood, West Hollywood Chamber of Commerce, and West Hollywood Design District BID, this book would not be possible without your imagination and investing in the magic.

Dear incredible humans of the hospitality industry, the bars, restaurants, hotels, and those creators of cocktails, your openness to participate has blown this project into a new stratosphere. It takes a lot to step into the unknown and trust me with your brand and recipes. Thank you for giving this book the ability to share your integrity and justice for your beloved brainchildren.

To everyone who I have spoken the words *Once Upon a Cocktail* with, whether you are an advocate, a collaborator, or maybe you declined participation, every conversation made this dream a realization. All your feedback made this book what it is and the book is eternally grateful, as am I.

Thank you all. May this be the beginning of many adventurous toasts!

Thank You's

A huge THANK YOU from both Sarah and I to everyone listed on this page. Without your support, this book would not have been possible. It took a village to pull this project off, the village of West Hollywood and many more.

Lexie Abner, Jason Abrams, Lou Adler, Jessica Agapetus, Max Ahumada, Kirsty Ainsworth, Nadia AL-Amir Galatro, Simone Alexander, Tanya Akim, Brian Allen, Charles Allen, Doreen Allen, Curtis Allmon, José Ambris, Victor Amezcua, Adrian Anchando, Janessa Andiorio, Cole Apodaca, Pano Argyriades, Austin Athouguia, Alexandra Azouz, Carmen Balasoiu, Ryan Barrington, Jen Bayless, Page Beaver, Alisa Berhorst, Troy Berry, Tammy Billman, Alexa Bird, Jen Bishop, Morgan Blanchard, Pauline Bonamigo, Chris Bonbright, Lisa Bonbright, Andrew Borenzwig, Greig Borthwick, Chris Brezina, Carol Bright, Kaitlyn Bronow, Daniel Brown, Douglas Bruchalski, Noah Bubman, Hannah Burkhart, Arcadio Cadena, Allan Camarena, Mike Camello, Rexx Cano, Derrick Carolina, Lawrence Carroll, Will Castillo, Patricia Catallo, Kayla Tobey Catherwood, Logan Rich Chabina, Albert Charbonneau, RJ Chesney, Devin Childress, Eric Cho, Gary Choi, Paris Chong, Milosz Cieslak, Serafina Clarizio, Kristin Clark, Cal Clarke, Gabriel Coble, Brandon Cohen, Max Cole, David Combes, Lyndsey Conrad, Chef Gabriel Contreras, David Cooley, Quinn Coughlin, Brian Cousins, Kristina Cox, Taylor Coyne, Brian Cranston, Nick Craven, Becky Crawley, Jennifer Crummett-Smith, Madeline Cutler, Karen Dailey, Charles D'Armetta, Harry Davis, Kelsey DeBrocke, Stephanie Delgado, Jordan Delgiudice, Aidan Demarest, Lisa DeMartino, Pamela Des Barres, Marissa Desilets, Jamison DeTrolio, Nick DeValk, Gina Devello, Lexie Di Chellis, Chris Diprete, Albertina Dominguez, Waldo Duarte, Stuart Duckworth, Sarah Eckert, Mark Edrington, Eddie Endo, John Erickson, Tim Erkelens-Probst, Devon Espinosa, Charles Essig, John Fab, Sara Fahlgren, Flint Faulkner, Michael Faulkner, Sebastian Felix, Gil Figueroa, Gregory Firlotte, Hans Fjellestad, Jessica Flanagan, Ricardo Flores, Milo Frank, James Frankie, Jon Frederick, Terrance Frederick, Courtney Freeman, Jo Gamez, Chris Garber, Jasmine Garcia, Desiree Gardea, Kelley Gattis, Melissa Gedney, Eric George, Cole Gerdes, Christina Gilmour, Marissa Glennon, John-Baptiste Godard, Josh Goldman, Ben Gomez, David Gonzales, Paulo Gorsse, Rod Gruendyke, David Gunning, Douglas Q. Hahn, Joe Hall, Alan Harden, Fiona Harden, K. Ryan Henisey, Justin Henry, Marissa Hermer, Matt Hermer, Rachel Madison Hill, Ryan Hook, Maryam Hooshim, Philip Howard, Angela Hughes, Nicci Hunter, Shawn Ilardi, Grace Iverson, Jason Jackson, Kamron Jafari, Cory James, Darian James, Nathan Jenisch, Stephanie Jerzy, Aaron Jimenez, Dave Jones (Jonzy), Gulla Jónsdóttir, John Jordan, Cydney Joseph,

Alexander Kardos, Chris Karmiol, Bill Karpiak, Tina Karras, Daniel Katona, Bonnie Keinath, Vanessa Kekina, Peter Kerr, Paolo Kespradit, Tom Kiely, Andrei Kissin, Justin Klinger, Kindall Kolins, Adam Koral, Matt Korpela, Michael Krajcar, Jeff Kulek, Elyse LaBrucherie, Sebastian LaCause, Rachel Lanphere, Brett Latteri, John Laun, John Leonard, Tony LePenna, Jessica Leslie, Jared Levy, Tyler Levey, Craig Ley, Polina Leytman, Deborah Lisboa, Jewels Long Beach, Felix López, Ruben López, Emilio Lourdes, Alfonzo Luna, Peter Madrigal, Katy Madzar, Lee Maen, Amy Maglieri, Mike Maglieri, Jeff Mahony, Isabella Mancebo, Cassie Marmas, Diego Marrero, Skyllar Marroquin, Aidan Marus, Erick Matos, Annie May and Kiki, Luis Mazariegos, Rhiannon McCollum, Rod McComber, Casey McShane, Mike Meldman, Mark Mengoni, Michelle Mertens, Todd Metzger, Melina Meza, Pam Michelsen, James Miller, Arnold Mina, Steven Minor, Natalie Mlynar, Mike Mohamed, Erin Mohr, Frank Moore, Maria Montgomery, Laura Moriarty, Genevieve Morrill, Jeff Morris, Cary Mosier, Phoebe Moyer, Chef Víctor Muñoz, Natassia Nazario, Hayley Nemeth, Kimberly Neville, Jonathan Nicholls, Tobi Nierob, Jennifer Oakley, Jordan Ogron, Shadi Omeish, Jason Oppenheim, Romy Orantes, Vanessa Orozco, Nicholas Ortega, Guido Ortuno, Laura Oudinot, Tracy Paaso, Jayke Padilla, Liam Parsekian, Manny Patel, Aaron Paul, Aaron Peaslee, Marco Pelusi, Caitlin Penny, Chamal Perera, Jill Peterson, Paul Joseph Piane, Szymon Piechaczek, Jason Pleskow, Jon Ponder, Harley Potter, Nathalie Pouille-Zapata, Conrad Pratt, Tim Pratt, Josh Pritchard, Bianka Radic, Liana Ragousa, Isaac Ramirez, Luis Ramos, Greg Rang, Mojie Rashtian, Joel Raznick, Maxwell Reis, Norbert Relecker, Chance Reno, Alan Rice, Nick Rimedio, Jasmine Rivera, Jackie Rocco, Mauricio Rodriguez, Brandon Romo, Karla Roque, Brian Rosman, Matt Ross, Robin Ruge, Joe Ruppert, Tobin Salas, Luis Saldana, Gill Sanchez, Nalani Santiago, Allison Samek, Aniesse Savo, Lynne Schacht and Johnny, Joshua Schare, Naomi Schimek, Tanya Sergei, Katherine Shadley, Tara Shadzi, Jacob Shaw, Ben Sheffield, Nick Shultz, Robert Silverberg, Eve Slaughter, Jason Slavkin, Grant Smillie, Kayla Smith, Lee Smith, Francesco Sorrentino, Jon Sotzing, Jamie Spies, Lily Stearns, David Stephenson, Sean Stewart, Jackie Subeck, Carolina Suero, Craig Susser, Kaitlin Sutherby, Ryan Sweeney, Robert Sylvia, Rohan Talwar, Cora Tang, Tash Tanti, Alex Tapia, Vincent Tapia, Randy Tarlow, Ashlea Tate, Michael Tebbe, John Terzian, Miyoshi Thahir, Dimple Thakkar, Evan Thomas, Noemi Torres, Lauren Trickett, Gary Trudell, Moses Truzman, Julian Tucker, Lucian Tudor, Johnny Uhorchuk, Julia Vagapova, Bruno Vergeynst, Ulysses Vidal, Carlos Villa, Ace Von Johnson, Suzie Vuong, Karlo Wabe, Tara Warden, Dale Warner, Jenna Webster, Chad Weiner, Dave Whitton, Sarah Willis, Jamie Wilson, Sally Wilson, Brandon Wise, Kelly Withers, Parker Wittbrodt, Heidi Wittekind, Katherine Wojcek, David Wood, Chad Yoho, Eddie Zammit, Guillermo, and Brett Zimmerman.

Foreword

A common misperception about Los Angeles is that as the second largest metropolitan city in the US, it's a massive place. And while LA is undoubtedly a big city, I like to describe it more like a quilt which is made up of several small squares that create the greater whole. As a local, you then choose one or two of your favorite neighborhoods, and that's where you spend ninety percent or more of your time. For me, West Hollywood is one of those destinations, a 1.9 square mile municipality known as The Creative City. It's where I spent six years at La Peer Hotel, which I opened in 2018, and where I served on several boards including Chair for four years of the West Hollywood Chamber of Commerce and Chair for three years of the West Hollywood Design District which is the neighborhood along Melrose, Robertson, and Beverly.

Being involved in so many organizations allowed me the privilege to meet truly amazing people—from the business owners and managers who make up the business community to their employees who bring those businesses to life, as well as city staff who work tirelessly to make West Hollywood a better place, and organizations like the Chamber and the West Hollywood Travel and Tourism Board who are its cheerleaders. I learned that West Hollywood is not just The Creative City, it's a personal city forged by genuine relationships and collaboration.

So I saw the potential for something really special when Katie Brightside first pitched me her idea for the cocktail book. Katie, who I've known since 2017, is a generous person as well as an accomplished artist. Her initial vision of creating a small cocktail book to help promote the city's bars and restaurants after the devastating effects of the pandemic was both heartfelt as well as captivating. Why captivating? Because I immediately envisioned capturing the magic of drinks at icons like the Tower Bar (Sunset Tower Hotel) or the Sunset Marquis, to local hotspots like Craig's, Cecconi's or Gracias Madre, to name a few. West Hollywood's restaurant and bar scene is so rich, vibrant, and diverse, I knew that the cocktail book could be much bigger than Katie imagined.

From there, I was all too happy to help with introductions and whatever Katie needed—whether it was another set of eyes or a sounding board. The most important piece that I added was to connect Katie with Sarah L.M. Mengoni, a legendary Kimpton mixologist and all around wonderful person, as I knew that the book had to have a legit mixology backbone. I was thrilled to see them become fast friends and better collaborators.

So, what you have in your hands is an incredible piece of art created by the loving genius of Katie and Sarah which represents the liquid art crafted by the best bartenders in West Hollywood's hotels, restaurants, and bars. It has been an epic journey for Katie and Sarah in developing this, and I salute them for the amazing gift that they have given us through *Once Upon a Cocktail*, which hopefully will stir joy in your glasses and home bars for years to come.

Written by Nick Rimedio | Co-Producer

Table of Contents

Preface

It's January 2023, and from the crest of The Sunset Strip, I am sitting at my computer listening to torrential rain, while fully in the weeds completing this cocktail book. I'm sitting here thinking to myself, what a year! Long gone are the balmy nights when Sarah and I traipsed all over West Hollywood looking for a drink. Not just any drink, we sought ones that quenched thirst and inspired the palette into summersaults. I am constantly filled with emotions as I recall memories of building the book. But here at my computer, bursts of the repeated word uttered by Hugh Grant's character in the opening scene of *Four Weddings and a Funeral* came to mind and were vocalized: "F**k!," what did I get myself into?! "This is an almighty project with many hats—and I am wearing them all.

It was in that sweet spot of calm, between the craziness of Christmas and New Year 2021, when I put the *Once Upon a Cocktail* pitch deck in front of Nick Rimedio, the former general manager of West Hollywood's La Peer Hotel. Nick has been a longtime friend and collaborator. In fact, it was quite normal for us to mull over ideas. LA was still in a pandemic hangover and slowly easing out of its shell. It felt like the right time for a city to come together to create such a project. Nick picked up his phone, and in a puff of magic, Sarah L.M. Mengoni arrived. "Katie, this is Sarah; she is our Lead Bartender here. Maybe she can help with the recipe book." With that effortless introduction, Sarah gave me her contact details, which were printed on an oval shaped beer mat. I thought, "I'm going to like this lass!"

A few weeks later, on a rainy night (it does rain a lot in January), we slid into a bar at happy hour (a bar that didn't make the book). After a few less-than-average Margaritas, we bar hopped, geeking out on what this book could be! This marked the beginning of a beautiful collaboration and friendship.

How did the *Once Upon a Cocktail* concept begin? We have to rewind back to the solo art exhibition, *My Fairytale Perspective on Love*, at the aMBUSH Gallery in Sydney, Australia on Valentine's Day 2012. The opening night was an extravaganza with various activations around my artwork's romance theme, including a *Love Potion* cocktail served from a caldron sponsored by Green Tree Absinth Fairy. This was my very first collaboration with a liquor company and in exchange I wove their Green Fairy logo into an illustration featured in the show. The exhibit portrayed several fairytale characters with a warped sensibility. Each personality had a split good and naughty persona, reflected as a two-piece artwork set.

The description read, "The Good: *Pixie Dust* – Tinkerbell and the Green Fairy lock lips in a magical kiss. All pixie dust and sparkles, their love has wings. But is the Green Fairy's glitter what Tinkerbell really wants?" And "The Naughty: *X Pixie Dust* – The Green Fairy rests his cheek on Tinkerbell's pregnant belly. Above the couple, Tinkerbell's children wait to be born. One is a mini-Tinkerbell and the other, a baby Peter Pan!"

In my artwork, I have been mischievously adapting fairytales for thirteen years. This underbelly narrative is thought provoking and allows me, as an artist, to play with traditional themes in contemporary ways.

Skip to 2017 (I promise it all makes sense from the 30,000 foot view of my life) when I landed my initial contract with Nick Rimedio. We produced an illustrated passport-size-book of landmarks and places to go within a mile radius of the La Peer Hotel. In addition, we wanted to highlight the city's historical creation; however, that part ended up tabled from the passport. A year later, I presented Nick with an extension to the passport project called the Design Bible, a full guide to the businesses in the West Hollywood Design District. This too was tabled. My next commission was for the City of West Hollywood. *A Turret Affair* was 600 feet of vinyl artwork that showcased along the wired fence of Santa Monica and Crescent Heights Boulevards. It was an idealization of architectural turrets. A turret is a small tower, typically set on top of a castle. In this project, I speculated that in West Hollywood we have more turrets per person per square-foot outside of France!

My following creative adventures specialized in hospitality design, branding, menus, murals, and wall art. I salivated over the opportunity to draw cocktail menus; my illustrations not only capture the spirit of the drink, but also the elevated experience of it in a glass.

With a few weeks free between projects, I noodled the infancy of *Once Upon a Cocktail* working with a few liquor companies. Like many self-initiated concepts, they are tabled when paid jobs arrive. It wasn't until the pandemic radio silence that I had time to shape a draft to completion. I shopped around the draft and reworked the layout until the penny synced and I passed that pitch deck to Nick in those closing days of 2021.

It was not just one project that led to this final version of *Once Upon a Cocktail*. It was a culmination of all the noted wins and tabled losses that fed this beast, combined with a huge dash of determination to make something stick.

Fast forward to the now and what this book has become. *Once Upon a Cocktail* captures the environment of a venue with its cocktail. This book is a tour-guide to drinking in West Hollywood, with an inclusive menu offering a-little-bit-of-something for everyone's palette. It is also so much more than a book for tourists. I've observed that we don't see our home city as does a tourist. As a one-time visitor turned deeply rooted resident, I lived the valuable twain perspective. With help from Sarah and our multitude of local partner businesses, we created a birds-eye-view of West Hollywood for both vantage points.

Once Upon a Cocktail is a treasured keepsake, a celebration of a plot of land's evolution. This is a book that reveres the past, the present, and our ever-evolving future. *Once Upon a Cocktail* tells what The Creative City, West Hollywood, was before it became the place it is today. It is a place we can step inside of to create and memorialize our personalized moments as they fall across our own timelines. Like us, this book creates its own space in history by interweaving the soul experience of a reader as a thread through the venues, their cocktails, and their creators—a tapestry of our shared story. The past, present, and future of West Hollywood and all our residents and guests co-exist in these 200 pages.

Since the journey began, the city gained many new watering holes that were unfortunately too late to squeeze into these pages; we also lost four venues that had originally signed onto the book (cocktails still included). I have learned that this too is evolution, especially in the hospitality industry. The ephemera of life is to toast the present, live fully, and repeat!

This impossible-possible project is finally realized. Please responsibly enjoy and know that love created it. Bottoms up! Katie x x x

Introduction

Thank you for purchasing *Once Upon a Cocktail*, a recipe book. It was created with much love and attention to detail. The rule book may have bent and twisted a few times in its creation, but for good reason. I hope explaining my approach here helps you understand why flexible rules were necessary. I will flip-flop between "we" and "I" a few times here and it's intentional; the "we" is something Sarah and I worked on together and the "I" is solely my bad influence.

The recipes throughout the book were carefully curated by Sarah to give a vast selection of drink profiles. There was no hard and fast process to this, especially in the book's infancy. However, there were three criteria that needed to be met before a cocktail landed on our page.

1. It had to be *really* good. Or a *really* good version of a simple classic.
2. It had to fit in the context of the book, balanced with the other concoctions.
3. It needed to accurately represent its venue.

For example if a bar was suggesting their signature cocktail (and they did), if it didn't fit one of these listed criteria, then you won't find it in this book. This doesn't mean that the drink was not up to par, it was, but it was not in keeping with the harmony of this book.

As a reader, you should expect to see a cocktail recipe that has passed the Sarah L.M. Mengoni standard and has been tested to make sure you can accurately recreate it at home. Whether you're a local with a night-in pajama party or back home from vacation, you can have a bar-away-from-bar nostalgic day or evening and recreate that good time on your own.

Recipe measurements are in ounces for consistency and accessibility for the home-creator. We have chosen not to have an ingredient list (whoops sorry) in the layout to engage the reader to observe all the preparation steps: The Wait, The Mix, The Process, The Fandangle, and most important, The Creator. It's important to read through an entire recipe before gathering ingredients or going shopping because there is often a wait period, and we would hate for you to rush out and buy ingredients that will not be used for a week. I also take full blame for these *seemingly* unorthodox preparation headings on the recipes. Back in 2018, I was obsessed with creating a recipe book with titles that were punchy, like a character name from *Reservoir Dogs* combined with the narration of Matt Berry's *Toast of London*. In the 2012 British Sitcom it was Berry's repetitive affectation of *Clem Fandango* that made me appropriate *The Fandangle*, what would otherwise be known as in a normal-ish book as *The Garnish*.

From the get-go, both Sarah and I had a clear intention for her voice to narrate the Tasting Notes. We felt her expertise as a mixologist and knowledge of cocktail history would best connect the reader to each cocktail, bar, restaurant, and hotel. This is not a normal practice for a recipe book, but ours is more than just recipes. We were creating something that helps readers decide where to visit or what to make and at the same time offer some insight into the history and culture of the enigmatic West Hollywood, making their experience more intimate. With Sarah's voice and perspective the reader could get a feel on what to expect. We also wanted the notes to read multiple ways—individually, in neighborhoods, and as a curated list—just like all the cocktails.

A glossary was included to provide you with additional information, definitions, and technique descriptions that may help you to better understand how to make the cocktails. If you're uncertain about a term, technique, tool, or glass that we've mentioned, you can look it up in one of its three sections: Glassware, Terms & Techniques, or Tools.

Naughty me assumed the West Hollywood map. To better serve the needs of the book, I designed some of the neighborhoods using a more expansive geography than the city's. The Design and Rainbow Districts more accurately follow the city's official designated area; whereas, City Center and Sunset Strip have both been drawn a little loosey-goosey to consolidate the catchment zone.

I have been obsessed with color-coding since I laid eyes on the London Tube Map—designed in 1933 by Harry Beck. I would say his design is a huge influence on why I color-coded the neighborhoods; it clearly identifies the separate sections in the book or on the WeHo map effectively (page 19).

COLOR KEY GUIDE

Design District **(DD)** | Turquoise   Rainbow District **(RD)** | Purple   City Center **(CC)** | Tangerine
Sunset Strip **(SS)** | Magenta   Life Hack **(LH)** | Kelly Green   Build Your Own **(BYO)** | Royal Blue

How to Use This Book

To reference and trace the location of each venue, bar, restaurant, and hotel on the map, they are represented by their corresponding page number in this book.

Each chapter begins with a featured writer who welcomes and leads us into the neighborhood. It was important to me that an expert encapsulates the spirit of that area. The Design District is presented by Gulla Jónsdóttir, a formidable Architectural Designer. David Cooley, owner of the legendary The Abbey Bar & Food, penned the foreword for the Rainbow District. The powerhouse, Genevieve Morrill, president and CEO of the West Hollywood Chamber of Commerce and the book's co-producer introduces readers to City Center. Sunset Strip's featured writer is the creative Hans Fjellestad, director of 2012 *The Sunset Strip* documentary. You've got me opening the Life Hack chapter because who else puts an IV drip in a cocktail book—well it is an IV cocktail—of vitamins and minerals! The Build Your Own chapter was an intriguing component that I was adamant about including, as the City of West Hollywood has been and continues to be on the forefront of expansive cannabis legalization legislation efforts. This chapter is brought to you by the pioneering Jackie Subeck, who is leading the change many want to see in our city, county, and state laws.

There are actually nine voices in total represented in this book. To conclude this list from above, we have Visit West Hollywood delivering a bar hopping adventure through our city's participating iconic hotels. Nick Rimedio, the book's co-producer, writes our Foreword. And finally, there is Sarah L.M. Mengoni, our fearless cocktail creator, and me.

Another short list of odd balls to expect along your journey through our recipes includes Hugo's, where we added both the Bloody Mary and Michelada. These drinks are almost the same but not. Their tomato mix recipe is decades old and honed to perfection. While at The London West Hollywood at Beverly Hills, both Sarah and I couldn't resist placing two cocktails, one of which features Seedlip Non-Alcoholic Spirit in the Panoma 94! The final curveball is the unexpected (spoiler alert) boozy cake recipe from Hotel Ziggy.

Like any good book we have a comprehensive index, which starts on page 191. And yes, I couldn't help myself: I COLOR-CODED it. The Key Guide can be found under the title. This key allows you to search by allocated color to the division of glossary, brand, liquor type, drink name, modifier, venue, or flavor profile. Please note, we have abbreviated some of the details to not fall prey to compromise and use a more diminutive font size. After a few drinks, if it were smaller, it would not be legible. Trust me; I had your eyesight in mind when we made that call!

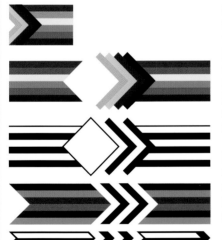

From *Once Upon a Cocktail's* conception, I wanted history nuggets that gave you information on what the venue was once upon a time. They are short-and-snappy. If you want to know more there is a Source List on page 190 and a link to whiz you off to a website complete with hyperlinks to support a deep dive into more detail. Sarah and I included a Timeline on page 21 that entwines the West Hollywood history research from Jon Ponder with Sarah's knowledge of historical drinking. We wanted a way for you to easily see how all of these fascinating moments relate and oftentimes influence one another.

It was suggested we tackle the conclusion together as a Q+A; after all, it is a cocktail recipe book containing sips of joy. With this style we could give readers some lively insight behind the scenes and a forecast into our future and next steps. This approach blended well with our sensibility to twist, bend, and break book traditions. Why not?!

Design is always in the details! Most creative books use icons and consistent visual language to express to the viewer an overarching feel for identity. I am a huge fan of strong branding and *Once Upon a Cocktail* endorses that. From my 2017, *Brightside Fairytale* handwritten font in the book's namesake, cocktail, and page titles—all those letters were painstakingly hand placed into position—to the quirky illustration style, page layout, and the page dividers, there is a reason and a rhyme for its existence. An example of this would be to look at the illustration above. I took the LGBTQ+ flag and broke it down into lines before stripping it back to create the page dividers. An arrow from that divider informs the icon adjacent to the page number.

To put it simply, there is not one corner of this book, designed with gusto, that hasn't been considered. With that, we are proudly presenting to you a thoughtful book that united a community over several drinks. Cheers!

Visit West Hollywood

It's pretty clear to those that know West Hollywood that the city is one part actual place and one part state of mind. West Hollywood vibrates with a virtual force field of creative energy, attracting and cultivating today's top trend-setters and visionaries to the small city for people who crave originality, appreciate innovation, revere artistry, and respect excellence.

Visitors and locals love how each of West Hollywood's diverse and walkable districts—Santa Monica Boulevard, Sunset Strip, and the Design District—each possess its own vibe. As you explore deeper into the districts you begin to find the hideaway bars ensconced inside West Hollywood's storied and luxurious hotels; they are as unique and inviting as the city itself. They are masterful art galleries creating bespoke cocktails, initiating conversations, and inspiring dreams.

A tropical oasis awaits you at the Sunset Marquis' Cavatina—where escapism is seen as a good thing.

Bring Fido, order a drink, and relax in an old Hollywood cozy garden hideout at The Chamberlain West Hollywood under a trellis.

Discover your new favorite cocktail at The West Hollywood EDITION hotel's Lobby Bar, a new kind of gathering place for travelers and locals alike.

Juniper Lounge at 1 Hotel West Hollywood employs ingredients from its own onsite organic garden and takes a seasonal approach to the syrups and juices they use to craft unique, delicious cocktails that will have you coming back for more.

Kimpton La Peer Hotel's lobby bar is an ideal spot to enjoy any number of cocktails, right in the heart of the infamous Design District.

An island bar, which is visible from the lobby, entices visitors at The London West Hollywood to gather amidst its casual opulence. The bar's understated luxury will inspire you with its taste-making design and startling textures.

Inspired by being located in the Design District, Le Parc on Melrose is where fashion and art meet music and film. Its vibrant interior is awash with locally inspired original artwork, bold details, and a clean, sophisticated architectural palette. Overlooking the West Hollywood horizon, Le Parc's Skydeck is an alfresco bar and lounge featuring plush cabanas and couch seating underneath the Southern California sky.

Mondrian LA's enduring allure transcends trends, inspiring a sense of invincibility and endless reinvention; its Skybar is a West Hollywood pillar for carousing all day and all night long.

Tonic is the perfect place to imbibe on delicious cocktails as you watch the sun set over the LA skyline at Montrose at Beverly Hills' rooftop pool-side bar.

Nature and art lovers will agree that there is nothing petite about Petit Ermitage, whose rooftop garden is recognized as a hummingbird and butterfly sanctuary and whimsical private art collection, displayed throughout the halls, showcases original artworks by the likes of De Kooning, Dalí, Miró, and more! BOLD. SOPHISTICATED. GLAMOROUS.

Bar Pendry patrons savor a plethora of visual candy at the Pendry West Hollywood, where classic cocktails meet moody vibes in the spot that once harbored the infamous House of Blues.

Not only one of the finest examples of Art Deco architecture in the Los Angeles region, the Sunset Tower Hotel was also called home by Hollywood royalty-Frank Sinatra, Marilyn Monroe, Howard Hughes, John Wayne to name a few.

In the heart of The Strip, Hotel Ziggy is where you can unleash your creative renegade and party like a rockstar. Chug an exclusive cocktail or grab a slice at B-Side Pizza, listen to vinyl being spun in the lobby, guests even have access to instruments and equipment and can create music with friends in Ziggy's Shred Shed.

Andaz West Hollywood is the quintessential iconic Sunset Strip hotel where countless rock legends have played and stayed. The hotel has been reimagined for a modern day sophisticated visitor while paying homage to its rock 'n' roll roots.

We conclude this trip on Route 66 at the Ramada Plaza by Wyndham West Hollywood Hotel & Suites onsite restaurant, kitchen24, which sports a contemporary interpretation of your favorite diner spot-dressed up comfort foods and strong cocktails.

Learn everything you need to know about where to stay, where to go, and what to do at visitwesthollywood.com

West Hollywood

KEY GUIDE | Distance from the WeHo *Neon Diver* to:-

Beverly Hills & Rodeo Drive | 1.7 Mile

Crypto Arena | 8.1 Miles

The Getty | 7. 8 Miles

Griffith Observatory 8.3 Miles

Hollywood Sign | 8.6 Miles

LACMA | 2.2 Miles

LAX, Theme Building | 10.6 Miles

LA Zoo | 11.1 Miles

Malibu Beach | 20.7 Miles

Muscle Beach | 10.8 Miles

Santa Monica Pier | 10 Miles

Universal Studio | 7.1 Miles

Venice Canals | 9.8 Miles

The Wisdom Tree | 7.1 Miles

HOLLYWOOD

HOLLYWOOD

WEST
HOLLYWOOD

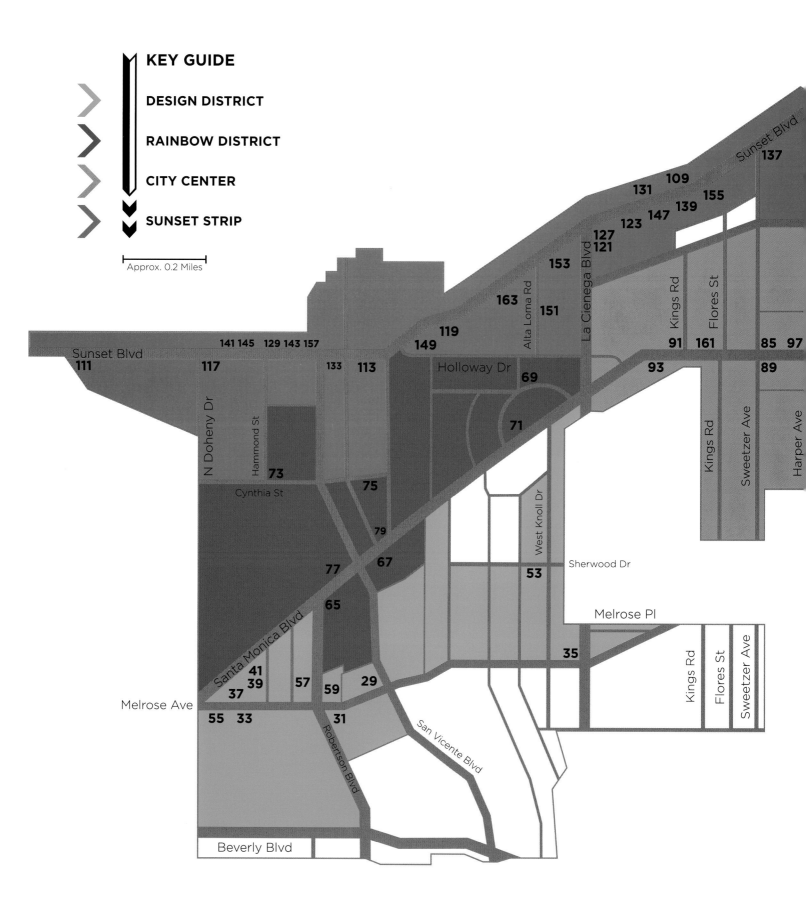

KEY GUIDE

DESIGN DISTRICT

RAINBOW DISTRICT

CITY CENTER

SUNSET STRIP

Approx. 0.2 Miles

The map number corresponds to venue location and the books page number.

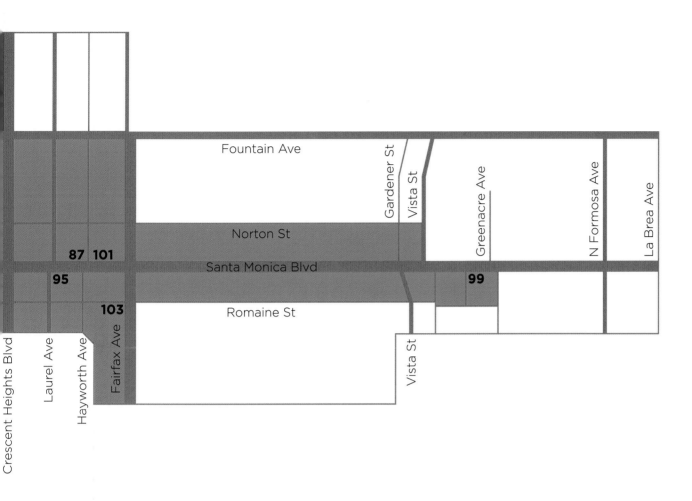

#		Name
29		Catch LA
31		Cecconi's
33		Craig's
35		E.P. + L.P.
37		Gracias Madre
39		Issima (R.I.P.)
41		La Peer Hotel
53		Le Parc at Melrose
55		Olivetta
57		Soulmate
59		SUR
65		The Abbey Food & Bar
67		Beaches WeHo
69		Chamberlain West Hollywood
71		kitchen24 (Ramada by Wyndham)
73		Montrose at Beverly Hills
75		Petit Ermitage
77		Stache
79		Trunks Bar
85		Conservatory (R.I.P.)
87		Delilah
89		Hamburger Mary's
91		Hugo's
93		La Bohème
95		Laurel Hardware
97		Norah
99		Phorage WeHo

#		Name
101		Surly Goat
103		Ysabel
109		Andaz West Hollywood
111		BOA Steakhouse
113		The Classic Cat
115		The DEN on Sunset
117		Lobby Bar (The West Hollywood EDITION)
119		Eveleigh
121		Harriet's
123		Hotel Ziggy
127		Juniper Lounge (1 Hotel West Hollywood)
129		Justin Queso's
131		Katana LA
133		The London West Hollywood at Beverly Hills
137		The Naughty Pig
139		Bar Pendry (Pendry West Hollywood)
141		Rainbow Bar & Grill
143		Rock & Reilly's
145		The Roxy Theatre
147		Skybar (Mondrian LA)
149		State Social House
151		Sunset Marquis
153		Tesse Restaurant
155		Tower Bar (Sunset Tower Hotel)
157		Warrior Bar (R.I.P.)
161		Earthbar
163		Next Health

Timeline

500 BC The Tongva people arrived in the region that will later be known as Los Angeles. They called the area Tovaangar. Over the next 2000+ years, more than 100 well-established villages emerged.

1769 A Spanish outpost was built in Tovaangar. Settlers soon followed, upending the Tongva people's way of life, enslaving many.

1806 First printed definition of the cocktail: "A stimulating liquor, composed of spirits of any kind, sugar, water, and bitters..." Over the next two centuries, the term evolved to refer to any concoction containing alcohol.

1810s Cato Alexander, a former enslaved person who had purchased his own freedom, became one of the first celebrity bartenders emerging in NYC.

1821 Mexico won its independence from Spain; California then became part of the First Mexican Empire.

1848 The United States annexed California from Mexico.

1850s Variations of the cocktail's original definition began to appear in print.

1856 The term *Mixologist* is invented for a humorous magazine story.

1860 Henry Hancock acquired Rancho La Brea, the parcel of land now encompassing West Hollywood.

1862 The first book devoted to cocktails is published in New York, Jerry Thomas' *Bon-Vivant's Companion.*

1864 Camels are Coming! West Hollywood's first settlers arrived leading a herd of camels. The camels lived in the marsh by Melrose Place and La Cienega Blvd.

1864 Nathan "Nearest" Green, an enslaved man, helped teach Jasper "Jack" Daniel distillation. Nearest, once freed, went on to be Head Distiller for Jack Daniel's Distillery in Tennessee. (SS | 141)

1874 The notorious bandit, Tiburcio Vásquez, is captured. He had been hiding for weeks at his friend, Greek George's, adobe (the first known dwelling in West Hollywood). George betrayed Vásquez to claim the $13,000 reward, then used the money to purchase Bolton Canyon, which later became the Hollywood Bowl.

1882 The Manhattan cocktail is first mentioned in print.

1883 Henry Hancock died. His West Hollywood land is inherited by his nephews, the Quint brothers. Greek George, former cameleer in the US Army's Camel Corps, released the animals to roam free in the hills.

1888 Sunset Blvd is first recorded in city documents.

1890 A trolley line is laid along Santa Monica Blvd through the Quint brothers' land. The trolleys stopped in the 1940s and the last transit train ran in 1965.

1891 First cocktail book written by a woman, Harriet Anne de Salis, is published, *Drinks a la Mode.*

1890s Belgian Victor Ponet built an estate on Sunset Blvd, north of Sunset Plaza Dr. The dirt road that crossed his land later became The Strip. His descendants, the Montgomerys, still own much of this land, which includes the famed Sunset Plaza.

1892 Industrialist Moses Sherman built a streetcar yard at corner of Santa Monica and San Vicente. This is where the Pacific Design Center, Bus Depot, and Sheriff Station currently sit. The Village of Sherman (coined after Moses) grew up around this yard and established West Hollywood's historic core.

1905 Ground is broken on a 140-acre development called Hacienda Park. Sunset Blvd extended by developers to what is now known as Sunset Plaza.

1906 Ponet's property is incorporated as part of the sprawling City of Sherman.

1914 Mary Phelps Jacob, also known as Caresse Crosby, patents the first bra pattern.

1917 The first cocktail book written by a Black bartender is published, Tom Bullock's *The Ideal Bartender.*

1919 Alla Nazimova bought property that is to become the infamous Garden of Allah. The hotel's launch party was held on January 9, 1927.

1919 Prohibition began in the US.

Referencing West Hollywood History and the History of Drinking.

1919 Moses Sherman campaigned to keep the expanding City of Sherman's name but lost by a bare majority vote in favor of the more glamorous, West Hollywood. For a while it was called by both monikers, until 1925, when it was universally considered just the latter by its locals.

1920 The 19th Amendment was passed by Congress on August 18th, granting women the right to vote, although universal suffrage did not extend to all women equally, especially in Southern States where women of color, immigrants, and impoverished white women were subjected to myriad tactics designed to suppress their voices.

1921 Sherman Chamber of Commerce was founded. In 1925, the board of directors changed its name to West Hollywood Chamber of Commerce (WHCC) to reflect the city's new name, and in the 1930s, the LaBrea Chamber merged with WHCC.

1922 Rudolph Schindler built a modern masterpiece of architecture, Schindler House, at 835 N Kings Rd.

1922 Mary Pickford and Douglas Fairbanks bought Jesse D. Hampton's original 1918 studio on Santa Monica Blvd and Formosa Ave; they named it the Pickford-Fairbanks Studio. It became United Artists in 1926, then later, The Lot at Formosa.

1927 The Hacienda Park Apartments are built; in the future they are renamed Piazza del Sol. (SS | 131)

1927 Drag Queen, Karyl Norman (George Paduzzi), billed as "the Creole Fashion Plate," performed at Sunset Plaza's Cafe La Bohème.

1928 Charlie Chaplin put out a fiery explosion at a Sunset Plaza speakeasy, The Russian Eagle. He doused the flames with a garden hose!

1929 The Sunset Tower came to life as a 46-unit luxury apartment house. (SS | 155)

1929 The Mojito's first print appearance, under the name Mojo de Ron, in Juan Lasa's Cuban publication, *Libro de Cocktail*. (CC | 99)

1930 Bruz Fletcher began his five year residence as society singer and pianist at the exotic, gay-friendly Club Bali on Sunset Blvd and Holloway Dr.

1930 At the Bubliche Cafe, Sunset Blvd and Larrabee St, the house balalaika orchestra played while acrobats juggled flaming daggers.

1933 Prohibition repealed in the US.

1933 The Clover Club on Sunset Blvd, housing a secret casino behind movable wall panels, became the most lucrative nightclub of its time. The club advertised itself as "Harlem in Hollywood."

1933 The *Vice War* appeared when Angelenos, who campaigned to stop illegal drinking, gambling, and prostitution on The Strip, doused two large mobile signs with kerosene and torched them.

1934 Don the Beachcomber opened in Hollywood, helping to usher in the Tiki craze.

1934 Billy Wilkerson, then publisher of the Hollywood Reporter, opened the French-themed Cafe Trocadero in Sunset Plaza.

1936 Route 66, established in 1926, is extended through West Hollywood's Santa Monica Blvd; it was decommissioned as a US Highway in 1964.

1937 Lee Francis ran an A-List bordello in the very building currently housing Katana LA. (SS | 131)

1940 Contruction starts on the streamlined Moderne (a style of Art Deco) building at 626 N Robertson Blvd, atelier to Fashion designer Daniel Werlé, who created clothing for actress Loretta Young.

1940 Billy Wilkerson's other late night supper club, Ciro's, opened. It is now the Comedy Store (1972), 8433 Sunset Blvd.

1940s The Moscow Mule is invented on The Sunset Strip by Smirnoff marketing genius, John Martin, and Cock'n Bull owner, Jack Morgan. (SS | 143)

1940s John Martin stayed busy after the success of the Mule by popularizing the Bloody Mary and the Screwdriver through continued creative advertising for Smirnoff. (CC | 91)

1940s Wilkerson builds the Flamingo in Las Vegas; this trend for city strips eventually led to less gambling and high end supper clubs in WeHo. By the 1960s, Sunset had a total facelift as a revolutionary music epicenter.

1942 The US military closed 62 gay bars in Los Angeles. Three were in West Hollywood, two bars and the lesbian Cafe Internationale in Sunset Plaza.

1944 Chef Joe Sheridan invented the Irish Coffee in Foynes, Ireland. (RD | 71)

1945 Many restaurants on The Strip are indicted by a grand jury for breaking meat rations, including Cafe Gala, Villa Nova (now Rainbow Bar & Grill), and Ciro's. The charges against all three miraculously vanished.

1948 The Bellini is invented by Giuseppe Cipriani for his Harry's Bar in Venice, Italy. (CC | 89)

1948 Mobster Mickey Cohen owned at least one legit business as a cover for his associates, the working man's bar, Continental Club, at 7825 Santa Monica Blvd. Later, it became an exercise studio, Training Mate.

1949 After Mickey and his gang closed Sherry's Cocktail Bar on Hammond St at four am, gunmen opened fire. Cohen was wounded, a bodyguard was not so lucky.

1951 Headlining Ciro's, burlesque striptease artist, Lili St. Cyr, featured her innovative on-stage bubble bath routine, where she's stark naked, except for a fur coat that gets seductively dropped. This sensational performance led to her arrest for indecent exposure on the show's second night.

1953 The Margarita, as we know it today, first appeared in print. (CC | 103)

1953 Local Hollywood Regency designer, Phyllis Morris, debuted her infamous Pink Poodle lamp.

1954 The Piña Colada is invented by Ramon "Monchito" Marrero Perez for the Caribe Hilton in Puerto Rico. (DD | 41)

1956 In order to sneak booze into an alcohol-free-zone Christmas party on an army naval base, Tom Lehrer poured vodka into orange jello. Thanks to Lehrer, every generation since has enjoyed the frat-house fave, Jello Shots. (DD | 45)

1956 Jack Nicholson's professional acting debut occurred at the Players Ring. (LH | 161)

1957 Dwight D. Eisenhower signed the Civil Rights Act on September 9th.

1959 Garden of Allah is demolished.

1960s The Pink Pussycat, a high class strip club at 7969 Santa Monica Blvd frequented by the Rat Pack, also housed the Naval Academy. (CC | 87)

1961 A theater at Santa Monica Blvd and Crescent Heights is reconfigured into P.J.'s Discotheque by Elmer Valentine. This is the first rock 'n' roll club in the whole of Los Angeles.

1964 Next, Elmer Valentine converted an old bank building into the infamous venue, Whiskey a Go Go.

1964 Sean Connery, starring as Ian Fleming's James Bond in Goldfinger, changed the Martini forever when he instructed the bartender to make his "shaken, not stirred."

1966 Buffalo Springfield is inspired by the Sunset Strip Riots to write *For What it's Worth*. The colloquially named *Youth Riots* were a revolt against municipal-imposed curfews, infringements of civil liberties, and for their right to gather in public. The conflict climaxed on Saturday, November 12, 1966. (SS | 115)

1967 The Factory, an exclusive nightclub opened in a building originally constructed in 1929 to manufacture motion picture cameras. Recently, it was demolished to make way for the Robertson Lane Project; it will be restored, piecemealed back to its former glory onsite.

1968 A women's liberation protest against the Miss World pageant on September 7 in Atlantic City was the first documented case of bra-burning.

1969 "I know this sounds like rock and roll fiction, but one evening I was with my main squeeze, Jimmy Page, waiting in front of the Hyatt "Riot" House on the Sunset Strip to go to the Led Zeppelin gig at the Forum when there was a massive crash. John "Bonzo" Bonham had tossed a huge TV from his balcony and it landed atop Jimmy's limo. It was too late to get another car so we climbed into the limo, trying to avoid the corner of the tv set that had actually crashed through the limousine's roof and rode to the Forum in rockin' Led Zep style." Pamela Des Barres, an original quote for *Once Upon a Cocktail* (SS | 109)

1970 The first LA Pride Parade was held on June 28, 1970. The parade moved to West Hollywood in 1979, five years before it officially became incorporated as an independent city.

1970 Andy Warhol films his underground movie, *Trash*, at Hotel Tropicana, which is now the Ramada by Wyndham (RD | 71). In 1972, Warhol produced *Heat* at the same location.

1970s In the early '70s, at the French Market, 7985 Santa Monica Blvd, gay people could dine out in the open, often for the first time. The building is due to be demolished but the historic patio will remain.

Brought to you by Sarah L.M. Mengoni, *Historically Drinking* and research from Jon Ponder, *West Hollywood History Center.*

1970s — Jungle Bird cocktail is invented for the Aviary Bar at the Kuala Lumpur Hilton. (page 172)

1971 — Mariano Martinez invents the first frozen Margarita machine for his bar in Dallas, TX. (RD | 67)

1971 — *LA Woman* was recorded by The Doors in the bathroom at 8512 Santa Monica Blvd, now Tail o' the Pup.

1971 — "I was not a big drinker the night Led Zeppelin had a party on the entire 6th floor of the Hyatt House, their favorite home away from home. Crates of Dom Perignon kept rolling in and not knowing my booze limits yet, I kept imbibing. I'd just learned how to read palms and was regaling Stevie Wonder about his excellent future when all four members of Zep sashayed into the room in full drag. That's the last thing I remembered before waking up in my own bed 24 hours later, unable to lift my head off the pillow. I still have no idea how I got home and I've never had another sip of Champagne since that wild night. Even the smell of it makes me dizzy." Pamela Des Barres, an original quote for *Once Upon a Cocktail* (SS | 109)

1972-ish — Hollywood legend has it that around this time on *The Tonight Show Starring Johnny Carson,* the famous host asked the First-Lady-of-American-Screen, Bette Davis, for advice on "...the best way an aspiring starlet could get into Hollywood." To which Ms. Davis replied without hesitation, "Take Fountain!"

1972 — The Rainbow Bar & Grill established itself as a rock 'n' roll institution when Alice Cooper, John Lennon, Ringo Starr, Keith Moon, Harry Nilsson, Bob Brown, and Micky Dolenz formed the Hollywood Vampires, at the time a drinking club. Their clubhouse eventually took over the Rainbow's attic space and afterwards, was affectionately called the Hollywood Vampires' lair. (SS | 141)

1973 — The Roxy Theatre began operating as a world class music venue. (SS | 145) A year later, The *Rocky Horror Show* made its first debut.

1973 — Sunset Marquis was home away from home for many rock legends. (SS | 151)

1975 — The Pacific Design Center's Blue Building was completed, the Green Building in 1988, and the Red in 2012. The iconic trio were designed by architects Cesar Pelli and Norma Merrick Sklarek for Gruen Associates.

1976 — Duke's Coffee Shop was listed by the LA Times as one of the great places to have coffee in Los Angeles. (RD | 71 & SS | 157)

1977 — The Source on Sunset Blvd and Sweetzer Ave was a pioneer in the health food movement. It was featured in Woody Allen's *Annie Hall*, where the onscreen Allen ordered, "alfalfa sprouts and mashed yeast."

1979 — Donna Summers released Sunset People.

1980s — Circus of Books broke boundaries selling adult gay porn at 8320 Santa Monica Blvd. Just behind the store was the infamous *Vaseline Alley* cruising spot.

1982 — Wolfgang Puck served us Spago at the former 1939 Cafe Gala, 8795 Sunset Blvd.

1984 — The City of West Hollywood was officially incorporated as an independent city on November 29, 1984.

1985-ish — UK bartender, Dick Bradsell, invented the Espresso Martini. (DD | 51)

1987 — Mötley Crüe released their hit song, *Girls Girls Girls*, which name dropped The Body Shop Sunset Strip, a strip club that has been full nude since the 1960s.

1990-ish — Bartender Julio Bermejo invented Tommy's Margarita; it's named after his family's San Francisco restaurant. (CC | 103)

1990s — Dale Degroff helped to popularize the Cosmopolitan (RD | 65) by putting it on the menu at the New York, A-lister frequented, Rainbow Room (not to be confused with West Hollywood's, Rainbow Bar & Grill).

1991 — David Cooley opened his coffee shop, The Abbey. (RD | 65)

1993 — The notorious Hollywood Madam, Heidi Fleiss, was a bi-weekly regular at the hosted club night, On The Rox, a private bar above The Roxy Theatre. (SS | 145)

1997 — Tina Karras arrived in WeHo with two suitcases, all the way from North Carolina. It was this move that led to her launching Tina's Vodka in 2021. (SS | 145)

2013 — The year that ended illegal gambling on The Strip, again, when Molly Bloom was arrested. Bloom operated a celebrity high-stakes poker ring. One of the hosted venues was the legendary Viper Room's basement, 2007.

2015 — Supreme Court ruled, in Obergefell v Hodges, that same sex couples have an equal right to marry. Love wins!

2023 — In the newly renovated Tower Records Building, Supreme opened its doors just after Valentine's Day.

2023 — This book arrives in divine time on the West Hollywood stage!

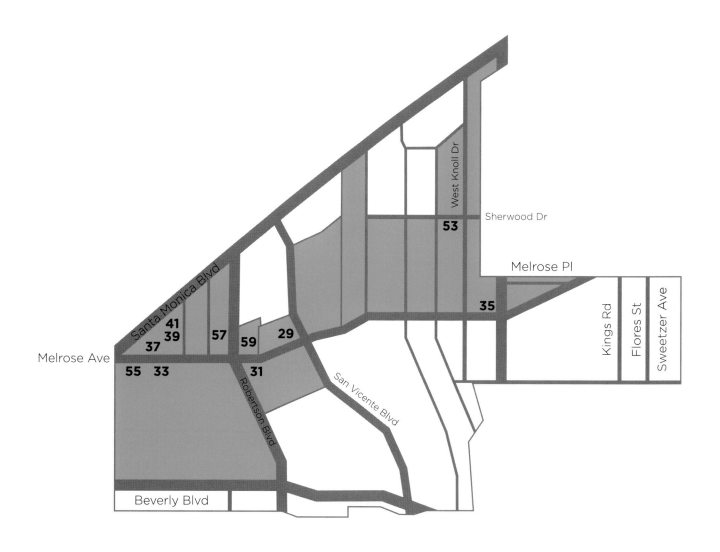

MAP KEY GUIDE | The map number corresponds to venue location and the books page number.

Catch LA **29** | Cecconi's **31** | Craig's **33** | E.P. + L.P. **35** | Gracias Madre **37** | Issima (R.I.P.) **39**
La Peer Hotel **41** | Le Parc at Melrose **53** | Olivetta **55** | Soulmate **57** | SUR **59**

Design District

Design District (DD) | Featuring Gulla Jónsdóttir

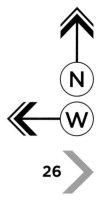

Gulla Jónsdóttir

Welcome to the West Hollywood Design District, a destination for all creatives where the vibrant neighborhood and eclectic hub of creativity, fashion, art, and design come to life. It is also the location of my Architectural studio; nestled between Beverly Hills and Hollywood.

My passion for architecture began when I was young; I knew that it was my calling. At the age of 19, I left Iceland and moved to Los Angeles to pursue my dream to study at Southern California Institute of Architecture. I was drawn to the innovative spirit and creative nature of West Hollywood. Nicknamed The Creative City, it has a unique energy that is unmatched by any other place I have visited in Los Angeles, and it keeps inspiring me to push the boundaries of my work.

I have been fortunate in my career; my work has traveled the globe. I've worked on renowned projects in the United States, Japan, Mexico, Iceland, Paris, Beirut, Bahamas, the Middle East, Greece, and China. No matter how far I go though, I always return home to the West Hollywood Design District. My international team and I have a passion for holistic work. We design across the fields of hospitality, commercial and residential design, museums, and wellness projects worldwide. This organic approach to design feeds into my unique line of limited edition furniture, which includes the *Petal Chair (see illustration).*

Over the years, I have had the pleasure of designing and creating many projects. One of my favorite projects is the La Peer hotel, located in this neighborhood. Believe it or not–it is also the same location I started my Architectural design studio back in 2009! But that is a funny story for another time, perhaps over cocktails at the La Peer...

The La Peer is a 105 room upscale boutique hotel. It evokes the heritage of the District, a space where art, music, fashion, poetry, film, and architecture commingle in spatial harmony. Created for both the neighborhood and its visitors, La Peer offers a comfortable hotel lobby and bar. The hotel's interior resonates with the pulse of our neighbors—from fashion and high-end furniture to studios of artists and poets in residence. An array of creative visitors gather here from all over the world and it all crescendos to arouse a sense of stylish curiosity. This lounge space is ready to welcome you into our diverse world of design. I still consider this boutique hotel my home away from home; it is an inviting place to have a cocktail or bask in the evening glow, watching the soft ripples on the pool.

But my work is more than creating functional buildings, hotels, and interiors for restaurants and residences. My work is a form of art, designed to evoke emotions, stimulate the senses, and inspire people. It's not just my beloved home; West Hollywood has given me the opportunity to grow as a designer and to share my passion with others. I have had the pleasure of working with some amazing people here, people that have helped me bring my visions to life, people who have become my good friends. I'm blessed to call so many in the Design District family.

Written by Gulla Jónsdóttir | Architectural Designer & Arts Chair of the West Hollywood Design District BID

I'm honored to be the Arts Chair of this District because it is a true melting pot of cultures and styles. You can feel the energy and excitement in the air as you walk down the streets. Always excited to see the changes and modern elements evolve here focusing on art, design, cocktails, and culinary destinations, I am delighted to share my West Hollywood Design District journey with you through some of the pages of this book; they are all places that I love to visit.

Created by Katie Brightside, this cocktail book is a tribute to the innovation that flows through this neighborhood. Design and cocktails are both about creativity. Indeed, they often inspire each other. I hope, as you explore the recipes and venues in this book, you discover the unique flavors, techniques, and people that make the West Hollywood Design District such a special place and I hope that you, dear reader, revel in a little taste of The District, the city that I love.

I couldn't imagine a more perfect person than Katie to create this book, as she's a radiant sunbeam, spreading warmth and joy wherever she shines.

Whether you are looking to impress your guests with a stunning cocktail or simply want to revisit your memories of the West Hollywood Design District at home, *Once Upon a Cocktail* is the perfect guide. So, pour yourself a drink and let the creativity of our incredible neighborhood inspire you!

Cheers and Love,
Gulla

gullajonsdottir.com

CATCH

8715 Melrose Ave.

The Nugget: Getting a reservation at Catch LA is like obtaining a key to the *Secret Garden*. Its entrance is a hidden passageway reminiscent of *The Lion, the Witch, and the Wardrobe*. Instead of a giant wardrobe, you access the otherworld of Catch LA through an elevator transporting you above West Hollywood.

The harmonious collaboration between nature and architecture starts with the 100 foot arched metal corridor entryway adorned with ivy and flowering vines. The theme continues with reclaimed beams and a 10,000 square foot retractable rooftop in the main dining room. Chris Kofitsas, of New World Design Builders, notes Catch as one of his notable works. "I wanted the experience to feel like you're in a garden, I always wanted a restaurant where you could dine among the flowers."

Catch came to New York City's Meatpacking District in 2011. Five years later its West Hollywood outpost opened with rave reviews. Catch Hospitality Group has grown into a multi-unit icon with two concepts, Catch and Catch Steak, with locations in major markets across the US.

8715 Melrose Avenue, a furniture showroom, was demolished in 2012 to make way for the restaurant reminiscent of C. S. Lewis' imagination. Catch LA opened in 2016.

Détox Rétox

The Prep:
Mint Syrup:
(Good for one month in the fridge, enough for eight cocktails.)
Put 4, loosely packed, tbsp mint in boiling water for 45 seconds;
pull mint from hot water and place in an ice bath.
Once it's cold, blend the blanched mint with ¾ cup simple syrup,
fine strain and then strain again through cheesecloth.

Juice and fine strain one lime (enough for one cocktail).
Juice and fine strain one English cucumber (enough for three cocktails).

The Mix:
2 oz Código 1530 Blanco Tequila
1 oz cucumber juice
.75 oz mint syrup
.75 oz lime juice
½ bar spoon matcha

The Process:
Combine all ingredients in a mixing tin and shake with ice.
Strain into a glass milk bottle (or a rocks glass).

The Fandangle:
Garnish with a cucumber wheel. Adding a striped paper straw is a great finishing touch!

The Creator:
The Catch Hospitality Group

DESIGN DISTRICT

CECCONI'S
West Hollywood

8764 Melrose Ave.

The Nugget: "Meet the badass women brigade of Cecconi's West Hollywood" reads the title of an article on the Soho House website. Not only was the leadership team all-female at the time, but so was the kickass bartender, Julia, who created Cecconi's famed Lychee Martini. When Sarah and I slid up to the bar and restaurant on R+D, it was refreshing to be in this unique situation in what is often a male-dominated arena. At the helm were general manager, Sara Fahlgren; assistant general manager, Jenna Webster; and floor manager, Hayley Nemeth, who together have created a supportive environment and encouraged creativity in their cocktail program along with the world-wide Cecconi's cocktail classics.

A big personal thank you to Cecconi's dynamic team for championing this project from its early conception.

8764 Melrose Avenue was originally a gas station in 1928 and was converted into a restaurant space in 1981, frequented by artists such as Ed Ruscha and David Hockney. Morton's took over the lease in 1994, before SoHo House's Cecconi's West Hollywood opened in 2009.

Lychee Martini

The Prep:
Juice and fine strain one lemon (enough for six cocktails).

The Mix:
2 oz Amass Vodka
.5 oz Soho Lychee Liqueur
.25 oz St-Germain Elderflower Liqueur
1 oz lychee juice
.25 oz lemon juice

The Process:
Combine all ingredients in a mixing tin and shake with ice. Strain into a coupe glass.

The Fandangle:
Garnish with a dehydrated lemon wheel.

The Creator:
Julia Vagapova

LIFE.!

Craig's

AN AMERICAN RESTAURANT

8826 Melrose Ave.

The Nugget: The infamous Casamigos, brainchild of George Clooney, Rande Gerber, and Mike Meldman, is the featured liquor in Craig's Danny Ocean Cocktail. Mr. Clooney starred as Danny Ocean, the protagonist in the 2001 Ocean's Eleven franchise. He has also been a champion of Craig's since their door swung open in 2011. Craig Susser, the restaurant owner, dedicated the cocktail to Mr. Clooney for all his support and friendship over the years.

8826 Melrose Avenue was built in 1950 and renovated as a restaurant in 1962. It was once home to the Dodgers Inn, Alberto's Yujean Kang's, Doug Arango's, and Melrose Bar and Grill.

Danny Ocean

The Boil:
Simple Syrup:
(Good for one month in the fridge, enough for six cocktails.)
Combine ½ cup sugar with ½ cup water and bring to a simmer.
Stir until the sugar is completely dissolved, then remove pan from heat.

The Prep:
Juice and fine strain one lime (enough for one cocktail).

The Mix:
2 oz Casamigos Reposado Tequila
.75 oz simple syrup
.75 oz lime juice
1 slice jalapeño
1 large basil leaf

The Process:
Combine all ingredients in a mixing tin and shake with ice.
Fine strain into a martini glass.

The Fandangle:
Garnish with a basil leaf.

The Creator:
The Craig's Team

WHERE LOVE LIVES

E.P. & L.P.
RESTAURANT & ROOFTOP

603 N La Cienega Blvd.

➤➤➤➤

The Nugget: Since 2015, 603 N La Cienega Boulevard is the birthplace of E.P. + L.P. (for Extended Play & Long Play) the first of many enterprises from The Botanical Group.

The rooftop bar shimmers with twinkling lights, a Hollywood Hills vantage, and a neon sign proclaiming this is *Where Love Lives*. E.P. + L.P. was designed and brought to life by the Australian firm Projects of Imagination.

The only historical research found on this site was for a 1946 building, home to David George Fabrics 1956–78. This property was demolished to make way for the new development that houses a collective of conceptual businesses—all pioneering in their own lanes.

Where Love Lives

The Prep:
Juice and fine strain one lemon (enough for two cocktails).
Cut two passion fruits (enough for one cocktail) in half,
using care to keep the halves together so you don't lose any of the contents.
Pour the contents into a fine strainer, pushing the liquid through with a spoon.
Discard seeds and keep the lovely thick liquid. This is your purée.

The Mix:
1 oz El Silencio Espadín Mezcal
.5 oz Yellow Chartreuse Liqueur
.25 oz Campari Aperitivo
.75 oz passion fruit purée
.5 oz lemon juice

The Process:
Combine all ingredients in a mixing tin and shake with ice.
Strain into a rocks glass half rimmed with tajin and filled with fresh ice.

The Fandangle:
Garnish with a lime wheel.

The Creator:
Milosz Cieslak

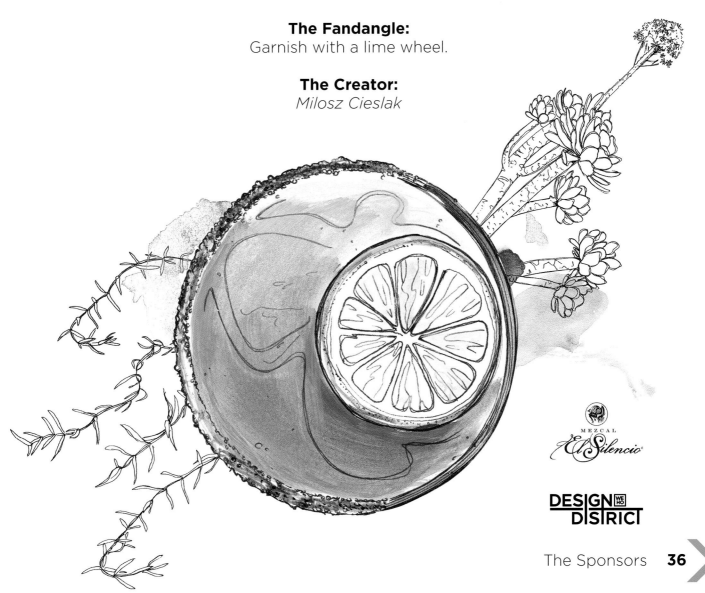

MEZCAL
El Silencio

DESIGN WEHO
DISTRICT

8905 Melrose Ave.

The Nugget: Gracias Madre was designed by the award-winning Wendy Haworth Design Studio in conjunction with architect, Victor Corona, and landscape designer, Scott Schrader, who transformed a simple parking lot into a luscious dining patio. The restaurant's setting is as intentional and exceptional as its food and beverage program with their sublime plant-based dishes and a strong agave mission #diffusethediffuser.

Former Bar Director, Maxwell Reis—one of those inquisitive, push-the-creative-boundaries cocktail enthusiasts—states: "The program at Gracias Madre was all about casually reshaping people's day to day perception about cocktails and agave spirits. My goal was to create things consumers can't make at home using cutting edge technology while creating less waste and an impressive product. Most importantly, it was about using ethically sourced and quality spirits that uplift the producers in Mexico and educate our guests on how to do that in their day to day lives."

8905 Melrose Avenue was built in 1941. Research shows it was an independent pet supply and grooming store, then a Petco brand store before becoming a gardening shop. Gracias Madre opened in early 2014.

Aguachili

The Wait:

Avocado Fat Washed Cascahuín 48 Plata Tequila:
(Good for two months, enough for twelve cocktails.)
Combine 1 cup and 7 oz Cascahuín 48 Plata Tequila and 4 oz full flavor avocado oil in a plastic
zip lock bag using the water displacement technique to remove all the air from the bag.
Next, sous vide the tequila/oil mix at 120 °F for one hour in an immersion circulator
(see Cocktail Terms and Techniques, page 183), agitating bag every 15 minutes.
Place the bag in freezer until the avocado oil solidifies,
then scoop out the frozen fat and strain the tequila through a coffee filter.

The Prep:

Aguachile Syrup:
(Good for seven days in the fridge, enough for six cocktails.)
Juice 2 cups of sliced cucumber, 1 ½ jalapeños,
and ½ cup, loosely packed, cilantro together, then add half the juice's final volume in sugar.
(For example, if you yield ½ cup of cucumber juice, you would add a ¼ cup of sugar).
Shake or stir until the sugar is completely dissolved.

Juice and fine strain one lime (enough for one cocktail).

The Mix:

1.5 oz Avocado Washed Cascahuín 48 Plata Tequila
.5 oz Kalani Coconut Liqueur
1.25 oz aguachili syrup
1 oz lime juice

The Process:

Combine all ingredients in a mixing tin and hard shake with ice.
Fine strain into a rocks glass over a large cube.

The Fandangle:

Garnish with a slice of jalapeño.

The Creator:

Maxwell Reis

DESIGN DISTRICT

issima

623 N La Peer Dr.

The Nugget: The cocktails at Issima were all created by one of LA's celebrated bartenders, Melina Meza.

"The concept of Issima came from the desire to create the feeling of being on a European vacation," says Melina. "Our beverage program brings this idea to life [by] using city destinations as our cocktail names. We wanted to focus on pairing fresh ingredients, native to the location, with different spirits to create eclectic vacation-worthy cocktails that our guests can enjoy all-year-round."

Issima (R.I.P.), a derivative of the Italian word bellissima, was located at 623 N La Peer Drive, inside the La Peer Hotel. During the pandemic, prior to Issima, the venue was home to its sister restaurant, Olivetta (DD | 55), which is now back in its intended location, 9010 Melrose Avenue. Viale dei Romani was the original restaurant in this open space when the hotel opened its doors in 2018.

Good news, Issima lives on and is relocating to the Thompson Hotel in Palm Springs to open late 2023.

Barcelona

The Boil:
Kiwi Basil Arugula Cordial:
(Good for one week in fridge, makes about seven cocktails.)
1.5 oz kiwi purée
¼ cup loosely packed basil
¼ cup loosely packed arugula
4 oz water

Combine basil, arugula, and water in a blender then blend for five seconds.
Empty blender into a small pot and add the kiwi purée.
Cook on medium until it comes to a boil, then remove from heat.
Fine strain when it's cool.

The Prep:
Juice and fine strain one Meyer lemon (enough for one cocktail).
Peel and cube three kiwis.
Purée in a blender then fine strain (good for one batch of cordial).

The Mix:
2 oz The Botanist Gin
.75 oz kiwi basil arugula cordial
1 oz meyer lemon juice
3 oz Fever-Tree Cucumber Tonic

The Process:
Combine all ingredients in a wine glass. Top with ice and stir for ten seconds.

The Fandangle:
Garnish with a basil blossom and petite basil leaves.

The Creator:
Melina Meza

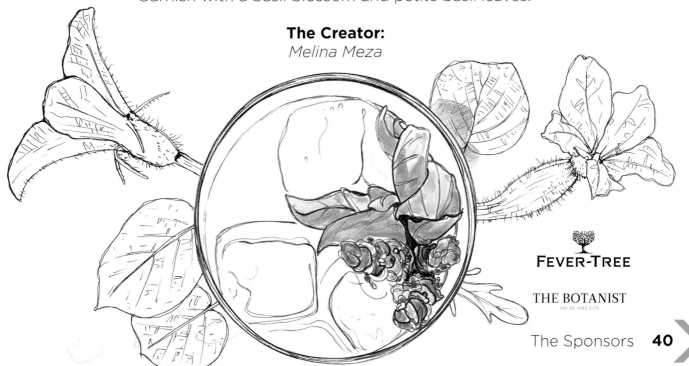

FEVER-TREE

THE BOTANIST
ISLAY DRY GIN

The Sponsors **40**

la peer hotel

627 N La Peer Dr.

The Nugget: In 1928, 627 N La Peer Drive sold waterproof stucco paint before becoming Au Frisson restaurant in 1962. By 2009 it housed Atelier Gulla Jónsdóttirs Architecture + Design Studio until it was bulldozed and reincarnated as the current hotel with her exquisite interiors.

The award-winning Jónsdóttir took the lease for four years knowing it would be demolished, while at the same time receiving the contract for the interior design on the future property.

With glowing reviews, the newly constructed La Peer Hotel, designed by architect Elizabeth Moule of Pasadena-based Moule & Polyzoides, was completed in 2017, with unique interior design by Gulla Jónsdóttir.

Whiskey Colada

The Prep:
Juice and fine strain one lime (enough for three cocktails).
Juice and fine strain ¼ of a pineapple (enough for six cocktails).

The Mix:
.75 oz Glen Grant 12 yo Single Malt Scotch Whisky
.75 oz Wild Turkey 101 Rye Whiskey
1 oz Kalani Coconut Liqueur
1.25 oz coconut cream
1.25 oz pineapple juice
.25 oz lime juice
1 dash Angostura Bitters

The Process:
Combine all ingredients in a mixing tin and shake with ice.
Strain into a tropical glass filled with fresh ice.

The Fandangle:
Garnish with pineapple fronds.

The Creator:
Sarah L.M. Mengoni

DESIGN DISTRICT

la peer hotel

627 N La Peer Dr.

>=====>>

The Nugget: Our cocktail curator, Sarah L.M. Mengoni, was the Lead Bartender at La Peer Hotel. Together, we wanted to add a few recipes as homage to the book's humble beginnings. The hotel's courtyard is where Sarah and I first met. Sarah has since departed on a cross-country adventure of a lifetime, and La Peer has continued to support Sarah's cocktail program. We would like to thank the La Peer Team and Kimpton Properties for helping us achieve our dream.

Misdirecting Travelers

The Boil:
Demerara Syrup:
(Good for one month in the fridge, enough for five cocktails.)
Combine ¼ cup demerara sugar with ¼ cup water in a saucepan and bring to a simmer;
stir until the sugar is completely dissolved and then remove from heat.

The Prep:
Juice and fine strain one lime (enough for one cocktail).
Juice and fine strain ¼ of a pineapple (enough for five cocktails).

The Mix:
1 oz Monkey 47 Gin
.5 oz Campari Aperitivo
.5 oz St. Elizabeth Allspice Dram
.5 oz demerara syrup
1.5 oz fresh pineapple juice
.5 oz lime juice

The Process:
Combine all ingredients in a mixing tin and shake with ice.
Strain into a highball glass filled with fresh ice.

The Fandangle:
Garnish with an orange peel.

The Creator:
Sarah L.M. Mengoni

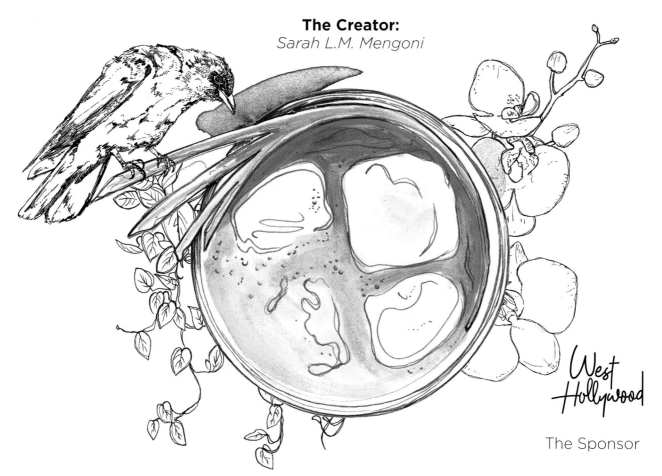

West
Hollywood

la peer hotel

627 N La Peer Dr.

The Nugget: "In the '90s jello shots were everywhere, often served in brittle plastic cups that you had to tongue out to consume," remarks Sarah. "It was clumsy, kind of gross, and sometimes the plastic would break and pinch your tongue. We all thought they were great! The more modern, elevated Daiquiri Jello Shots were part of a 1990s nostalgia cocktail menu I created for the La Peer bar. My mission was to create something that was sophisticated to ingest, vegan, and tasted like an actual cocktail."

Where did jello shots originate from before becoming a frat house staple? There are several claims, including one medieval not-quite-a-shot. Wine was used in this old-world recipe. Its acidity drew the gelatin from the animal bones and skin and contributed to making the stock and added flavoring. According to Ken Albala, the author of *The History of Food*, there have been recipes with booze and powder gelatin since it was invented in 1845. Another claim comes from Tom Legrer, who in 1956 would sneak boozy jello into the alcohol-free-zone Christmas party on an army naval base. Orange jello with vodka was his winning combination.

Vegan Daiquiri Jello Shot

The Boil:
Simple Syrup:
(Good for one month in the fridge, enough for one batch.)
Combine ½ cup sugar with ½ cup water and bring to a simmer;
stir until the sugar is completely dissolved and then remove the pan from heat.

The Prep:
Cut five limes in half from end to end. Score around the edges of the limes with a knife,
then scoop out all of the pulp leaving just the shell. Save that pulp and the shells!
Using a tool with a sharp rounded edge, such as a peach pitting spoon or a triangle corer*,
scrape out as much of the white pith as you can from the shell.
Take care to not tear or make any holes in the shells.
Juice and fine strain enough of the saved pulp to get 1.5 oz of lime juice.
see onceuponacocktailweho.com for example

The Mix:
(makes twenty shots)
3 oz water
1.5 oz lime juice
2.5 oz simple syrup
⅔ tsp agar agar
½ pinch salt
2 oz Appleton Estate Signature Rum
1 oz Kalani Coconut Liqueur

More Boiling:
Combine water, lime, simple syrup, and salt in a saucepan and bring to a simmer.
Slowly add the agar agar while stirring constantly.
Once mixed, remove from heat and add the Appleton and the Kalani; stir. Let cool for 15 minutes.

The Wait:
Pour mix into lime shells and put in the refrigerator for an hour and a half or until properly set.

The Process:
After the jello is completely set, cut each of the ten lime shells
into halves with a sharp knife to make twenty individual shots.

The Creator:
Sarah L.M. Mengoni

la peer hotel

627 N La Peer Dr.

The Nugget: Everything about this award-winning American whiskey brand, Beverly High Rye, is homegrown. When Sarah, and I began this journey we wanted to balance the known brands with local start-ups—it became a mission statement for *Once Upon a Cocktail*.

"A local brand often reflects the place where it was created and is often started by people who love their community," affirms Sarah. "Support given is support returned. As the brands grow, they often bring jobs, attention, and local pride up with them."

The founder of Beverly High Rye, Andrew Borenzweig, is a California native. He lives in our neighborhood and with his elevated whiskey celebrates the defined luxury that is West Hollywood's adjacent friend, Beverly Hills.

Without hesitation, Andrew joined our band of merry sponsors with the cocktail Working Title created by Sarah.

Working Title

The Mix:
1 oz Beverly High Rye Whiskey
1 oz Catoctin Creek Aged Peach Brandy
.5 oz Meletti Amaro
.25 oz Luxardo Maraschino Liqueur
1 dash Fee Brothers Barrel Aged Bitters

The Process:
Combine all ingredients in a mixing glass and stir with ice.
Strain into a rocks glass over a big ice cube.

The Fandangle:
Garnish with a skewered cocktail cherry
and cherry wood chip smoke from a smoke top.

The Creator:
Sarah L.M. Mengoni

THE
BEVERLY
HIGH RYE

la peer hotel

627 N La Peer Dr.

The Nugget: The original godfather of artisan mezcal was born in 1995. Like a god, Del Maguey's birth was presented to the world with fanfare. With both tequila and its cousin mezcal made from agave plants, today's gold rush is an agave plant rush.

"Del Maguey was the brand that introduced craft cocktail bartenders to mezcal in the early 2000s. It remains today as not only a popular brand, but also a leader in espousing traditional methods of production and in making a strong commitment to supporting and honoring the people who make it," explains Sarah. "Del Maguey's mezcals aren't made in factories, as some brands now are, they're made in a handful of very small, family distilleries located in Mexico's most charming villages."

We are honored to have them onboard.

Savage Journey

The Mix:
.75 oz Del Maguey Vida Mezcal
.75 oz St-Germain Elderflower Liqueur
.75 oz Salers Gentiane Apéritif

The Process:
Combine all ingredients in a mixing glass with ice and stir.
Strain into a Nick and Nora glass.

The Fandangle:
Garnish with an orange peel.

The Creator:
Sarah L.M. Mengoni

DEL MAGUEY
SINGLE VILLAGE
MEZCAL

la peer hotel

627 N La Peer Dr.

The Nugget: This cocktail was inspired by a model, maybe even a supermodel, who requested "something to wake me up, then fuck me up." The original Espresso Martini was created impromptu in the 1980s by celebrated bartender Dick Bradsell while at Fred's Club, London.

"Popular cocktails from the 1990s are seeing quite a resurgence," states our expert, Sarah, "and the Espresso Martini may be the leader of the surge. I've created many versions of this modern classic, but for La Peer we stuck to just a very slight variation of the much-loved original. We also added an option which is quickly gaining popularity, switching out the vodka for an aged tequila."

Turn Up

The Mix:
1 oz Grey Goose Vodka
OR
1 oz 818 Añejo Tequila
1 oz Caffè Borghetti Espresso Coffee Liqueur
1.5 oz espresso

The Process:
Combine all ingredients in a mixing tin and shake with ice.
Strain into a coupe glass.

The Fandangle:
Garnish with espresso beans.

The Creator:
Sarah L.M. Mengoni, from the classic recipe by Dick Bradsell.

THIS IS OUR HAPPY PLACE

love

leparc

733 W Knoll Dr.

The Nugget: Built in 1972 as a three-story apartment building, Knollwood House included a recreational tennis court on the roof. Until the City of West Hollywood built the marvelous Aquatic and Recreational Center, Le Parc had one of the only roof courts in WeHo.

The building was transformed into a hotel in 1979. Today, Le Parc has many things to celebrate including the artwork by Charlie Edmiston, Scott Hile's "LOVE" mural, and the recent interior design refresh by Waldrop+Nichols Studio.

To appreciate the full spirit and glamor of Le Parc, take in the city skyline poolside while sipping on the 1542 craft cocktail, made with what most of the Hollywood elite drank during prohibition, gin!

1542

The Boil:
Simple Syrup:
(Good for one month in fridge, enough for ten cocktails.)
Combine ½ cup sugar with ½ cup water and bring to a simmer;
stir until the sugar is completely dissolved, then remove pan from heat.

The Prep:
Juice and fine strain one lime (enough for one cocktail).
Juice and fine strain one cucumber (for a few cocktails).

The Mix:
1.5 oz Old Harbor 1542 Gin
1 oz cucumber juice
.75 oz lime juice
.5 oz simple syrup
1 large slice of jalapeño

The Process:
Put the jalapeño in a mixing tin and muddle.
Add other ingredients and shake with ice.
Double strain into a double old fashioned glass half rimmed with tajin and filled with ice.

The Fandangle:
Garnish with a sliced cucumber on a skewer.

The Creators:
Tobin Salas

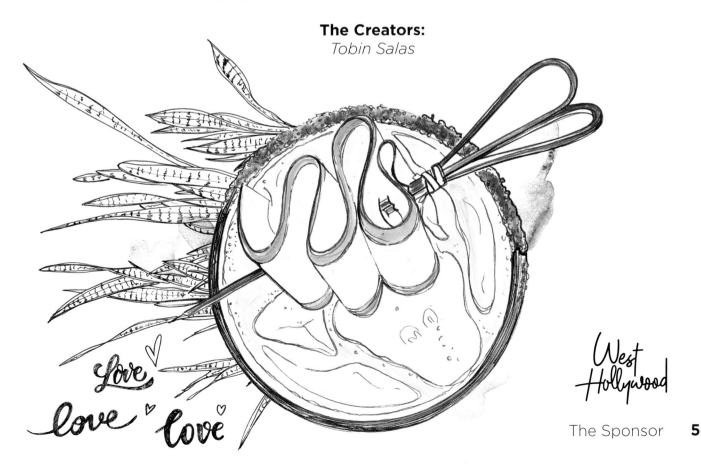

Olivetta

9010 Melrose Ave.

The Nugget: Created by Boujis Group, Olivetta's stellar interiors are designed by Tom Parker of Fettle, who commissioned illustrator, Alam Ellis, to create the custom wallpaper.

As an advocate and creator of bespoke wallpaper, I particularly agree with Tom's statement in Architectural Digest (Feb 2020), "I always think it's the sign of a decent place if someone has considered the restroom." It's often the little things that get overlooked, but owners Matt and Marissa Hermer have left no stone unturned with their attention to detail. It's those details that go a long way in a city of artists and dreamers.

Melina Meza's inventive bar program reflects the desirable atmosphere. "Designed to both be paired with our Mediterranean inspired dishes and to be enjoyed on their own," states Melina, "our cocktails are as beautiful to look at as they are delicious to sip on."

Book a reservation, grab yourself a cocktail, and transport yourself to another world.

Built in 1942, previous tenants of 9010 Melrose Avenue have been Café Figaro, Kass Bah, Parisian Room, Santo Coyote, Murano, The Artichoke's Heart, Smoke, and Au Fudge.

Dirty Blue Martini

The Prep:
Make the olive brine and infused dry vermouth first (enough for five Martinis).

Kalamata and Castelvetrano Olive Brine:
(Good for one month in fridge.)
Combine 1.5 oz kalamata olive brine
with 1.5 oz castelvetrano brine
and fine strain.

Gorgonzola Infused Dry Vermouth:
(Good for two weeks in fridge.)
In a blender, combine ¼ tbsp of gorgonzola cheese with 3 oz of dry vermouth.
Blend for five seconds and fine strain.

The Mix:
2 oz Grey Goose Vodka
.5 oz kalamata and castelvetrano olive brine
.5 oz gorgonzola infused dry vermouth

The Process:
Put all ingredients in a mixing glass
and stir with ice until the ice just barely starts to sink into the liquid,
roughly thirty seconds; strain into a coupe glass.

The Fandangle:
Garnish with skewered kalamata and gorgonzola stuffed olives.

The Creator:
Melina Meza

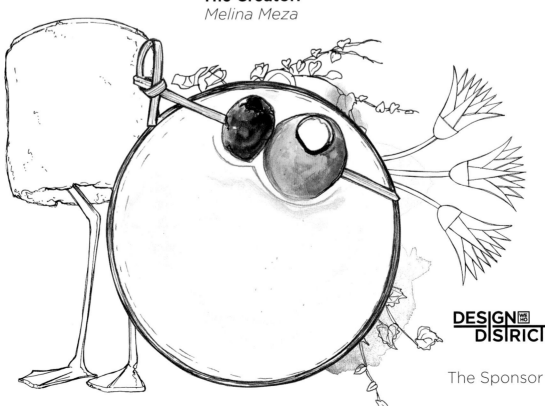

DESIGN DISTRICT

Soulmate.

631 N Robertson Blvd.

The Nugget: Soulmate has a driving force in design with Kelly Architects and Sean Leffers Interiors. Leffers uses organic living elements that give soul to the space. They commissioned artist, Santiago Quesnel, to document a journey from Buenos Aires to Los Angeles. This visual research informed the must-see, thirty-foot, scenic oil on canvas artwork in the restaurant.

Naomi Schimek, Soulmate's Bar Director, shows no lack of imagination with her approach to the cocktail program. "I like fabricating simple, natural cocktails to technical perfection as well as working with tropical nuances and all kinds of herbs and local flora," says Naomi. "Lately, what interests me is manicuring leaves and discovering new ways to create garnishes out of California native plants."

631 N Robertson Boulevard was a private residence during World War II, owned by Major Joseph D. O'Hanlon. In 1958 the property became a garage for sports cars and in 1967 was used by a company that specialized in British and exotic car repairs.

Soulmate

The Wait:
California Bay Leaves:
If you can get your hands on some California bay leaves,
clean them first and then leave them out to dry for one or two weeks.
If you can't find them, use traditional dried bay leaves.

The Boil:
Bay Laurel Syrup:
(Good for one month in the fridge, enough for eight cocktails.)
Put 8 whole dried bay leaves into ¾ cup of water that's just about to boil.
Remove from heat and let steep for thirty minutes.
Add ¾ cup of sugar and stir until the sugar is dissolved and then strain.

The Prep:
Juice and fine strain one lemon (enough for one cocktail).

The Mix:
2 oz Amass Dry Gin
.75 oz bay laurel syrup
.75 oz lemon juice

The Process:
Combine all ingredients in a mixing tin and shake with ice,
fine strain into a coupe glass.

The Fandangle:
Garnish with a dried bay leaf.

The Creator:
Naomi Schimek

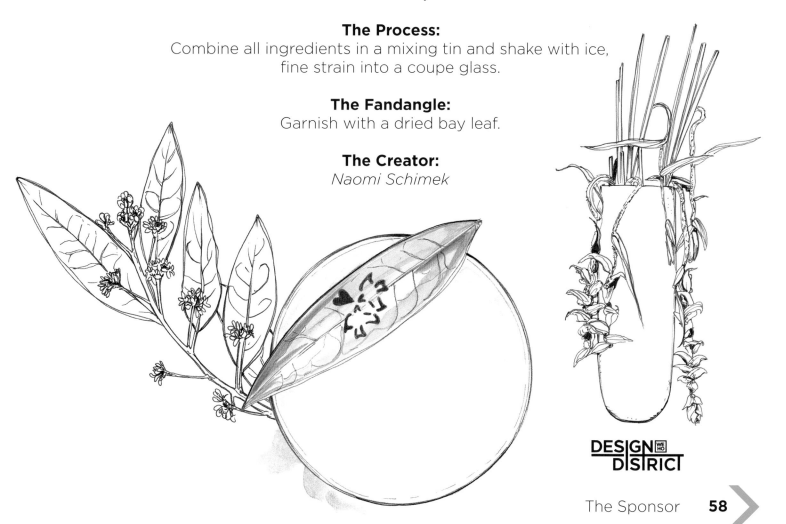

DESIGN DISTRICT

SUR
RESTAURANT
LOUNGE

606-614 N Robertson Blvd.

The Nugget: In the words of Oscar Wilde, "Life imitates art far more than art imitates life." The notorious writer adds, "the self-conscious aim of life is to find expression."

SUR means south in Spanish. The restaurant opened in 1998 with a humble beginning before finding fame through a hit TV show. Juxtaposed to its bashful start, a few tables, and whitewashed walls, the restaurant today can be found full of expression and pizazz, displaying an Aladdin's cave of worldly treasures.

SUR found a fresh resurgence recently with a new food (don't worry they still serve their infamous fried goat cheese balls) and beverage program enticing a broad spectrum of clientele.

SUR has been extended over time onto two properties, one built in 1931 and the other in 1947. 606-614 N Robertson Boulevard has been home to Baha'i Faith Group, Chryssanthou, The Helena Newland Gallery, Dog Groomer Bowser Boutique, Margo Leavin Gallery, Gagosian, and a Donna Karan clothing store.

The Rainbow

The Prep:
Juice and fine strain one lime (enough for one cocktail).
In a blender, purée 5 oz of strawberries
(makes about ½ cup purée, enough for six cocktails).

The Mix:
2 oz Veev Açaí Spirit
.75 oz lime juice
.75 oz strawberry purée
2 basil leaves
2 strawberries (remove stems and leaves)

The Process:
Muddle strawberries and basil in the mixing tin, add all other ingredients,
and shake with ice. Double strain into a rocks glass filled with fresh ice.

The Fandangle:
Garnish with two basil leaves and a strawberry.

The Creator:
Paulo Gorsse

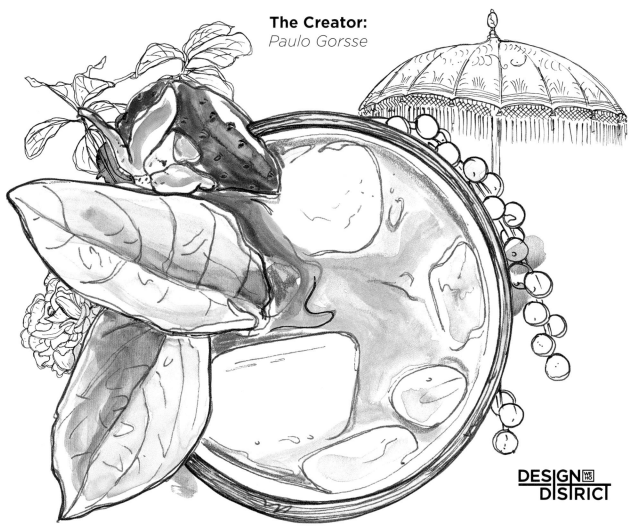

DESIGN DISTRICT

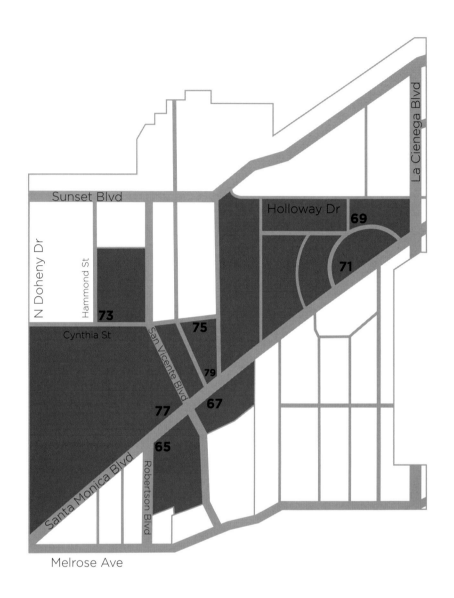

MAP KEY GUIDE | The map number corresponds to venue location and the books page number.

The Abbey Food & Bar **65** | Beaches WeHo **67** | Chamberlain West Hollywood **69**
kitchen24 (Ramada by Wyndham) **71** | Montrose at Beverly Hills **73**
Petit Ermitage **75** | Stache **77** | Trunks Bar **79**

Rainbow District

Rainbow District (RD) | *Featuring David Cooley*

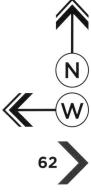

David Cooley

Welcome to West Hollywood! We are so glad that you are here to celebrate what our beautiful city has to offer. I am David Cooley, owner of The Abbey Food & Bar and The Chapel. I moved to West Hollywood in 1981 with a degree in Hotel Management from UNLV and a dream to open my own business. I chose West Hollywood as a city to live and for business because it was a place where I could be my authentic self and live openly and freely as a gay man. West Hollywood provided me comfort, a sense of community, and became a home where I could make lifetime friends who became family. In 1991, I was able to make my dream of being a business owner come true.

For over three decades I've watched the City of West Hollywood evolve like a growing tree. West Hollywood has always been a forward-thinking city, filled with excitement and entertainment. Many of the visitors who have come to West Hollywood, and now call it home, have added more value, diversity, and beauty to the fabric that makes it the great city I know and love to this day. It wasn't long ago that the city I call home only had a handful of gay bars and establishments like Motherlode, Micky's, and Blue Parrot-unlike what we see today in our vibrant and ever-changing Rainbow District. Through all my travels to LGBTQ+ destinations around the world, West Hollywood's Rainbow District remains one of the most robust and welcoming communities I've seen. Our Rainbow District is more than just LGBTQ+ establishments, boutique hotels, restaurants, and small businesses. West Hollywood has become a world class destination for famous events like Elton John's AIDS Foundation Academy Award Party, Emmy parties, Grammy parties, and Fashion Week.

Thanks to the community's embrace of a little coffee shop called The Abbey that opened on Robertson Boulevard in the early nineties, I've been able to see The Abbey grow to what it has become today–a world-renowned restaurant, bar, and nightclub. For three decades The Abbey has meant a lot of things to a lot of different people. Many times, customers have told me that The Abbey has been their very first gay bar experience. From children coming out to their parents, parents coming out to their children, people meeting for the first time and then getting engaged, hearing those personal stories are the biggest compliments I can ever receive. When you're going to The Abbey you never know what surprises may happen or who you'll see. We've enjoyed hosting celebrities like Christina Aguilera, Lady Gaga, Paula Abdul, Mariah Carey, and Billy Porter, to having pop-up concerts from Belinda Carlisle, Kim Petras, Rita Ora, and the legendary Diana Ross. The Abbey was even the late Elizabeth Taylor's favorite pub and the portrait she gifted remains on the wall in her honor.

Written by David Cooley | Owner of The Abbey Food & Bar

In 1981 I took a risk on relocating to a new city with just a dream and later opened The Abbey. I furthered my dreams when we've had opportunities to expand the footprint to serve our patrons, friends, and family in the best ways we can. Since the doors opened in 1991, we've grown from 1,100 square feet to the current 18,000 square feet that includes six bars and two dance floors with world renowned DJs, everyone has been to The Abbey's VIP and I see that sentiment returned from the city each year. The little coffee shop that I opened on Robertson Boulevard in the early nineties has now grown into more than just a daytime destination for coffee with friends, it's become a safe space and go-to destination for the LGBTQ+ community and our allies.

The Abbey and I have celebrated and endured so many memorable moments with the community of West Hollywood both in times of joy and in times of need. Our community fought the AIDS epidemic and discrimination and comforted each other when our nation has rolled back hard-fought progress for the LGBTQ+ community. Since the beginning, The Abbey has always been an active member in our community working together to organize and mobilize change. In 2012, The Abbey took a stance on banning bachelorette parties during the fight for marriage equality and was there to celebrate the historic milestone of marriage equality becoming the law of the land.

I've been so proud to have hosted events, meetings, and fundraisers for so many people and organizations like Human Rights Campaign and OnePULSE Foundation, to politicians like Pete Buttigieg, Hilary Clinton, state, and national elected officials and even our country's first woman Vice President, Kamala Harris, who advocates for LGBTQ+ people. Our annual traditions like Christmas in September, benefitting Children's Hospital Los Angeles, and the World AIDS Day Christmas Tree Lighting Ceremony, benefitting the Elizabeth Taylor AIDS Foundation, are some of the most meaningful moments I look forward to every year.

I'm also proud of The Abbey family who continue to be the foundation, along with the City of West Hollywood, that keeps The Abbey together. In 1981 I decided to take a chance on the unknown and make a home in a city that made me happy and proud of who I am, and I'm happy and proud to say that West Hollywood is still the place I love to call home and is where my Hollywood dream came true.

theabbeyweho.com

692 N Robertson Blvd.

⟩⟩⟩⟩

The Nugget: "Come as you are," is owner David Cooley's ideology at The Abbey. His is a gay bar where everyone is welcome, including non-gays. The Abbey, *this abbey*, provides a sacred safe harbor for the LGBTQ+ community and its allies. Whether to drink coffee, grab a tasty bite, or dance your butt off, The Abbey is a space where all people can coexist in community–it's a comfortable place where you can be whoever you want.

The Abbey opened in 1991 as a coffee and dessert shop located directly opposite from its current site. In recent years, that space was home to Bossa Nova before time made way for the Robertson Lane Project.

In 1994, Cooley leased the original 1936 building across the street that had sold oversized statues. In fact, he purchased many of those sculptures before the store closed; they grace The Abbey's décor today. The coffee shop's vision expanded even more with the golden ticket, a liquor license. The property has grown several times over the years, including an extension of the club in 2016 called The Chapel!

The Abbey is widely known as the 'best gay bar' in the world.

Cooley Cosmo

The Prep:
Juice and fine strain one lime (enough for one cocktail).

The Mix:
1.5 oz vodka (citrus infused is a great choice)
.5 oz triple sec
.75 oz cranberry juice
.5 oz lime juice

The Process:
Combine all ingredients in a mixing tin and shake with ice.
Strain into a coupe glass.

The Fandangle:
Garnish with an orange peel.

The Creator:
*This recipe is a modern classic whose origins are disputed by cocktail historians.
The "Cooley" in the name references the owner of The Abbey, David Cooley,
who played a key role in bringing the modern cocktail scene to West Hollywood.*

City of West Hollywood
California 1984

Beaches weho

8928 Santa Monica Blvd.

The Nugget: In an article on The Rise and Fall of Disco the author suggests 'Miami never received the memo that disco was dead, so it became a proud bastion of the genre'.

Beaches WeHo reinvigorates the lust of kitsch design and Latin flavors in their homage to '80s Miami disco culture.

8928 Santa Monica Boulevard was built in 1935. It was renovated from a retail space to a restaurant in the early 2010s and prior to that may have held the keys to all the broken hearts as a locksmith shop.

Beaches is one of a few venues in West Hollywood to host Cherry Bomb WeHo nights: weekend parties for women and gender-expansive people.

Mango Tango Frozen Margarita

The Boil:
Simple Syrup:
(Good for one month in the fridge, enough for four cocktails.)
Combine ½ cup sugar with ½ cup water and bring to a simmer;
stir until the sugar is completely dissolved and then remove the pan from heat.

The Prep:
Juice and fine strain two limes (enough for one cocktail).

The Mix:
1.5 oz blanco tequila
.5 oz Cointreau Orange Liqueur
1 cup frozen mango chunks
1 oz lime juice
.5 oz agave
4 oz ice

The Process:
Put all ingredients in a blender, and blend!
Add very small amounts of water if it's too thick. Pour into a hurricane glass.

The Fandangle:
Garnish with an edible orchid flower and a flamingo stirrer stick,
if you happen to have one lying around...

The Creator:
The Beaches WeHo Team

City of West Hollywood
California 1984

COINTREAU

chamberlain
WEST HOLLYWOOD

1000 Westmount Dr.

➡➡➡

The Nugget: Start off your trip or vacation with a celebratory glass of champagne! The ritual toast dates back to 6th century Greece as an offer to the gods for good health. Skip forward a few hundred years to Shakespeare's Britain, when the wine was a little acidic, where stale toast was dipped into the libation to absorb its acidity. The phrase stuck.

The word chamberlain derived from Middle-English and portrayed a person who was chief officer of a household to a noble or king or as someone who serves as a bedchamber attendant for a lord or sovereign. The building at 1000 Westmount Drive was constructed in 1976 and renovated in 1986, opening as Le Dufy Hotel in 1987. It was named for French impressionist Raoul Dufy and was rebranded as Chamberlain in 2005.

Since 2019, the hotel has had many things to toast—especially an interior overhaul that employed the exquisite taste of Jacqueline McGee of Perkins+Will Studio. The fresh décor was inspired by old Hollywood folk who often owned a *pied-a-terre*. With fashion as emphasis, the walls are covered with design illustrations.

Author's note: don't worry, this hotel has on-suites; there is no need for an actual chamberlain!

Perrier Jouët

The Prep:
Fill a champagne bucket halfway with ice and a bit of water.

The Process:
How to safely open your bottle of Perrier-Jouët Champagne:
Remove the foil that covers the cork and the cage.
Make sure the top of the bottle isn't pointing towards your face,
a loved one, or a cherished object; then place your thumb on top of the cage
and wrap your fingers and hand tightly around the neck of the bottle.
With your other hand twist the wire that's holding the cage six times away from you,
this will release the cage. Without removing your thumb make sure that the cage is loose.
Now with the same hand that loosened the cage, grab the bottom of the bottle and twist.
You'll feel the cork start to release itself, control it with your thumb until it's all the way out.

The Finish:
Pour yourself a glass and put the remainder of the bottle in the ice bucket.

West Hollywood

8575 Santa Monica Blvd.

The Nugget: Built in 1946, the Tropicana Motel and Dukes Coffee were hit by the wrecking crew in 1987. Dukes relocated up to The Strip at 8909 Sunset Boulevard and the beloved treasures of "The Trop's" hidden secrets were crushed forever. Tom Waits talks about the motel in a 1987 LA Times article calling it a "$9-a-night, music-industry hobo place where rock 'n' roll met Nathanael West—a kind of ranchette *manque*, pop-culture landmark haunted by the ghosts of Jimi Hendrix, Janis Joplin and others and immortalized on celluloid by Andy Warhol in '*Trash*.'"

Another Warhol underground movie, *Heat*, was filmed at the Tropicana and Duke's Tropicana Coffee Shop, which was listed among the greatest places to have coffee in Los Angeles in 1976.

Since 1989, the Ramada by Wyndham hotel has sat on the land that after 2011, also included kitchen24. An article in the LA Times states that kitchen24 was designed with a 'style is no style' aesthetic. Kristofer Keith at Spacecraft Group created the flamboyant décor with Neapolitan ice-cream colors and LED flying saucer lights.

Irish Coffee

The Mix:
2 oz Tullamore D.E.W. Original Irish Whiskey
1 oz St. George Nola Coffee Liqueur
1 oz Blackwelder Espresso

The Process:
Pour all ingredients into a small brandy snifter and stir.

The Fandangle:
Garnish with high quality whipped cream.

The Creator:
The kitchen24 Team

West Hollywood

IT
WAS
ALL A
DREAM

MONTROSE
AT BEVERLY HILLS

900 Hammond St.

The Nugget: The Montrose name originates from a town in Angus, Scotland; it is also an aristocratic title. Tellingly, the lead liquor in The Montrose's signature cocktail is Dewar's Scotch whisky!

900 Hammond Street was built as an apartment building in 1976 and transitioned to a hotel in 1983 as Le Valadon. Renovated in 2018 by Jacqueline McGee of Perkins+Will Studio, it was rebranded with the regal name, Montrose.

"I've always been driven by what I call 'design with a capital D,' that is, design that makes a difference," said McGee for myinspireddesign.com.

For this hotel, McGee drew inspiration from Hollywood's past and present entertainment industry, using a bold color palette with a rock 'n' roll sensibility.

If you're a fan of the *Queen's Gambit* check out the giant chess board on the rooftop, in the tennis court space.

Untitled

The Prep:
Fill a small atomizer with Green Chartreuse.

The Mix:
2 oz Dewar's White Label Scotch Whisky
1 oz Averna Amaro
2 dashes orange bitters

The Process:
Put all ingredients in a mixing glass and stir with ice until the ice
just barely starts to sink into the liquid, roughly thirty seconds. Strain into a coupe.

The Finish:
Spritz Green Chartreuse on top of the cocktail.

The Fandangle:
Garnish with a dehydrated lemon wheel and a sage leaf.

The Creator:
Tobin Salas and Sarah L.M. Mengoni

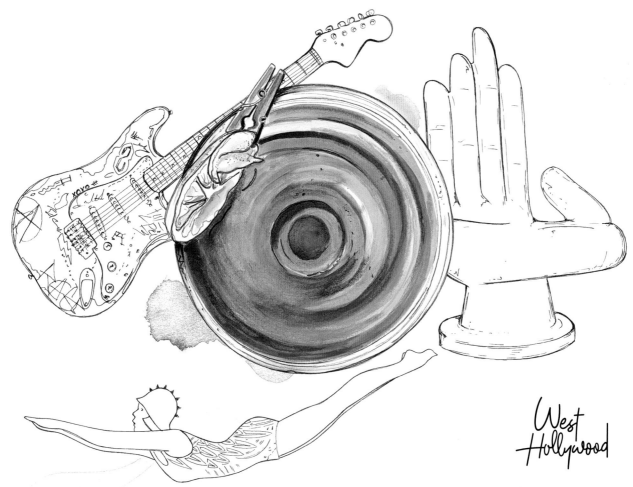

West
Hollywood

8822 Cynthia St.

Petit Ermitage

The Nugget: The double entendre, Belle de Jour, establishes the enigmatic feeling of the hotel with an aura of discretion. The name translates as both 'beauty of the day' and 'morning glory,' with the latter referring to the flower as it unfurls into full bloom under the rising sun (the phrase is also its own double entendre as it's slang for a man's morning fulsome, nudge-nudge wink-wink).

In the 1967 film *Belle de Jour* by provocative filmmaker Luis Buñuel, the exquisite Catherine Deneuve plays a bored bourgeois Paris housewife. Her lust for life had no spark until Catherine's character Séverine finds erotic liberation in moonlighting as a high-end courtesan. Séverine is given the call-girl name Belle de Jour, as she can only work in the day between 2-5pm.

Whether you're drinking the Belle cocktail or you're lucky to stay in the Belle Suite, bask in the sun and find your own liberation.

Originally built in 1979 as an apartment building called Le Reve, the property was converted into a hotel in the 1990s. Since 2007 it's been the euphoric Petit Ermitage.

Belle

The Boil:
Grenadine:
(Good for one month in the fridge, enough for eight cocktails.)
Mix 4 oz of pomegranate juice, 4 oz of sugar, and 1 pinch of salt in a small pan.
Bring to a simmer; stir until the sugar is completely dissolved
and then remove the pan from heat.

The Prep:
Juice and fine strain one lemon (enough for two cocktails).

The Mix:
.5 oz Laird's Bottled-in-Bond Apple Brandy
.5 oz Bénédictine Liqueur
.5 oz grenadine
.5 oz lemon juice
2 oz brut Cava

The Process:
Combine all ingredients, except Cava, and shake with ice.
Strain into a coupe glass; top with the Cava.

The Fandangle:
Garnish with skewered apple slices that have been dipped in lemon juice,
to prevent browning.

The Creator:
Sally Wilson

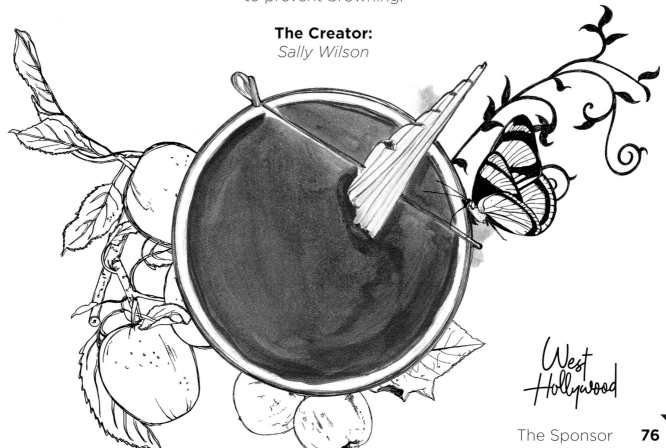

West
Hollywood

stache

8941 Santa Monica Blvd.

The Nugget: 8935 Santa Monica Boulevard was built in 1923. In the 1950s, it housed a bar called Barrel followed by a high-end French restaurant called L'Etoile before Café d'Etoile took reign for 36 years. Stache opened in 2021.

The name Stache derives from the word mustache, recalling the iconic '70s and '80s facial trends amongst gay men. The name is both a celebration of the LGBTQ+ community's resilience and a tribute to those who died with AIDS.

All the hand-crafted cocktails at Stache are named after songs, including *Somebody to Love* by the Queen of mustache's himself, Freddie Mercury!

Somebody to Love

The Prep:
Ginger Syrup:
(Good for two weeks in the fridge, enough for ten cocktails.)
Peel and chop an 8 oz piece of ginger. Run ginger through a juicer;
(if you have to use a blender add just enough water for the ginger to blend).
strain the juice and combine with the amount of sugar equal to the liquid output
(for example if you get 4 oz of ginger juice you would use 4 oz of sugar).
Stir or shake until the sugar is thoroughly dissolved.

Green Juice:
(enough for 5-6 cocktails, any you have left over drink the same day while it's fresh!)
Fine strain then combine the following:
1.5 oz cucumber juice
1.5 oz celery juice
1 oz kale juice
.25 oz turmeric juice
1.5 oz filtered water

Juice and fine strain one lemon (enough for two cocktails).

The Mix:
2 oz Casamigos Blanco Tequila
.75 oz ginger syrup
1 oz green juice
.5 oz lemon juice
2 dashes Scrappy's Fire Tincture

The Process:
Combine all ingredients in a mixing tin and shake with ice.
Strain into a rocks glass over ice.

The Fandangle:
Garnish with Bulls Blood Micro Greens.

The Creator:
Conrad Pratt, Sebastian LaCause, and Quinn Coughlin

City of West Hollywood
California 1984

SCRAPPY'S BITTERS

TRUNKS

8809 Santa Monica Blvd.

The Nugget: Invoking the words of Gloria Gaynor, "I am what I am," Trunks is a true West Hollywood gem of a gay dive bar. With no air and graces, good times flow in its free pours.

8809 Santa Monica Boulevard was built in 1923. In a *Los Angeles Times* article from 1935, there is reference to the location as a beer parlor, but likely without its frequently topless bartenders of today (it wouldn't be West Hollywood without a little objectification of willing subjects who have signed a 1099)!

Casamigos Mezcal Shot

The Wait:
Invite your closest friends over for a magical night of comradery.

The Prep:
Enjoy the satisfaction of removing the cork
from your brand new bottle of Casamigos Mezcal.

The Mix:
Line up small glasses for each friend in attendance,
pour 1 oz of the Casamigos Mezcal into each.

The Fandangle:
Garnish with an orange wedge.

The Creator:
Casamigos Mezcal is made in Oaxaca,
Mexico by a family, four generations deep, of Mezcaleros.

City of West Hollywood
California 1984

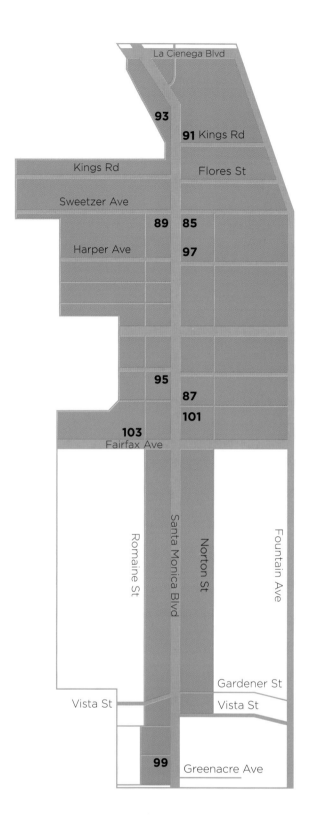

MAP KEY GUIDE | The map number corresponds to venue location and the books page number.

City Center

HISTORIC
CALIFORNIA
US
66
ROUTE

Emser
TILE

City Center (CC) | Featuring Genevieve Morrill

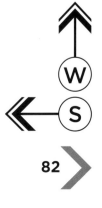

Genevieve Morrill

In 1999, I came to West Hollywood to work with the new owner of the Pacific Design Center as its Vice President. After a few years of serving on the West Hollywood Chamber of Commerce (WHCC) Board of Directors, the Board successfully talked me into assuming the role of its President and CEO. Under my leadership, the Chamber's influence in the community and its value for members has been significantly elevated.

You may ask, why is the President and CEO writing the foreword to West Hollywood's City Center? Simply, the West Hollywood Chamber of Commerce sits right in the heart of City Center.

I was talking to an executive from a large shopping center who described to me his experience of West Hollywood; he explained that when walking from Los Angeles towards West Hollywood, he and his clients knew immediately when they crossed the border. "It was a feeling," he said, "there was no border indicated, but you just knew something had shifted. You knew you had entered a special place." Welcome to West Hollywood! It's not just a place, it's an experience, an emotional connection, a romance, a celebration-it's nothing short of something truly special.

In general, West Hollywood is a beacon for unique boutique shops, innovative startups, and internationally recognized brands. We are The Creative City where dreams can come true, an entrepreneur can realize their vision, trends become viral, and innovations are celebrated. It is a place where international corporations anchor their headquarters and entertainment, hospitality, and retail brands open flagship locations-all to capture the West Hollywood brand magic that assists their business' success. It's not a secret that West Hollywood is the most valuable incubator for test marketing an exciting new concept.

City Center is the heart of West Hollywood. By definition, *center* is a place in or around which an activity takes place or from which something begins. This cozy neighborhood area has beautiful tree-lined streets and an extensive mix of architecture spanning from the 1920s, to Midcentury Modernism, and Spanish Colonial; it is also home to the historic Schindler's House. It touts the largest population concentration in West Hollywood; one-fifth of the city's 34,000 residents. Its west-east boundaries are La Cienega Boulevard and Fairfax Avenue. City Hall is located here, and a myriad neighborhood-serving businesses. You can see now why it's called City Center!

At the western border of City Center, a beacon of the old established restaurants, La Bohème stands tall. At this neighborhood favorite, you slide into an exquisitely upholstered booth that sports low lighting and baroque décor to enjoy a meal with a local flare. Their outside patio is a tribute to the new, contemporary, but cozy feel, with eclectic furniture and charm. Another local favorite is the much-loved diner, Hugo's, which shares a past beyond West Hollywood's cityhood. A butcher shop in the 1940s, the diner was established in 1975. If Hugo's walls could talk, the wealth of historic moments could fill bookshelves.

City Center is very walkable and has that quiet neighborhood feel, while still vibrating with creative energy. Business here spans from established legacy to innovative new–where you can hit one of the first of its kind cannabis consumption lounges like The Woods, which opened in 2022, after dropping off your dry cleaning at Holloway Cleaners, serving the community for fifty years. Or, grab a burger, a bellini in a leg cup, and have some fun at Hamburger Mary's Drag Queen Bingo Brunch! If burgers aren't your thing, vegan-out at Pura Vita, while getting your dog groomed next door before heading to your favorite realtor to scope out your forever home next to that!

Whatever your venture, business or leisure, West Hollywood opens opportunities for treasured moments, great experiences, and your wildest dreams coming true.

wehochamber.com

8289 Santa Monica Blvd.

CONSERVATORY
WEST HOLLYWOOD

The Nugget: Life's a Beach when you have to say goodbye to Sex in LA. We lost another great venue at the end of 2022, The Conservatory (R.I.P.). Even though they are gone, thank goodness, with their recipe safely recorded here, we can now enjoy Sex in LA at home with the added benefit of Postmating local favorite, Irv's Burgers, at the same time!

8289 Santa Monica Boulevard was built in 1947. The original occupant was an automobile repair shop with an onsite burger stand. Locals suggest it was Queenie's Burgers, then Joe's Burgers, before it became the iconic home to Irv's Burgers shack in 1950. Irv's was legendary with rock royalty and was immortalized on Linda Ronstadt's 1978 album cover, *Living in the USA*. The property was redeveloped into Beach Nation in 2014 and then again in 2018 for The Conservatory.

Sex in LA

The Wait:
Double Bubble Infused Reyka Vodka:
(Good for one month in the fridge, enough for four cocktails.)
Combine 8 oz Reyka Vodka with 4.5 oz Double Bubble bubble gum.
Store in an airtight container for 48 hours then strain.

The Prep:
Juice and fine strain one lime (enough for one cocktail).

The Mix:
2 oz Double Bubble-infused Reyka Vodka
.5 oz Giffard Lichi Li liqueur
.5 oz cranberry juice
.5 oz lime juice
3 dashes plum bitters

The Process:
Combine all ingredients in a mixing tin and shake with ice. Strain into a small carafe.

The Fandangle:
Fill a coupe with cotton candy and sprinkle edible glitter over it.
Pour the contents of the carafe over the cotton candy, then drink!

The Creator:
Chef Víctor Muñoz and Felix López

City of West Hollywood
California 1984

Delilah

7969 Santa Monica Blvd.

➡➤➤

The Nugget: *My, my, my, Delilah!* What a provocative past 7969 Santa Monica Boulevard has had. Since 2016, Deliah has been home to h.wood's modern-day supper club, which pays homage to the roaring '20s with exquisite interior design.

In 1935 the location housed a used-car dealership, Dolly's 20th Century Bowery, Seville's, Peanuts, Grand Ville Nightclub, Voyeur, and DBA. The latter four all individually pushed the boundaries of art, striptease, and burlesque.

The most infamous of them all was Pink Pussycat, which opened in 1961 and lived into the late '70s. During the day, the Pink Pussycat moonlighted as an adult-education center. Time magazine once reported that the curriculum taught classes such as *The History and Theory of the Striptease* and *The Psychology of Inhibitions.* Girls could major in everything from *Applied Sensual Communication to Dynamic Mammary, Navel, and Pelvis Rotation.* Time portal, please; sign me up!

The Toto

The Boil:
Simple Syrup:
(Good for one month in the fridge, enough for ten cocktails.)
Combine ¼ cup sugar with ¼ cup water and bring to a simmer;
stir until the sugar is completely dissolved and then remove pan from heat.

The Prep:
Juice and fine strain one lemon (enough for one cocktail).

The Mix:
1.5 oz Sunny Vodka
.5 oz St-Germain Elderflower Liqueur
.25 oz simple syrup
.75 oz lemon juice
4 strawberry wedges
prosecco

The Process:
Muddle strawberries in a mixing tin; add all ingredients, except prosecco,
and shake with ice. Fine stain into a coupe glass and top with prosecco.

The Fandangle:
Garnish with a skewered cocktail cherry.

The Creator:
Adam Koral

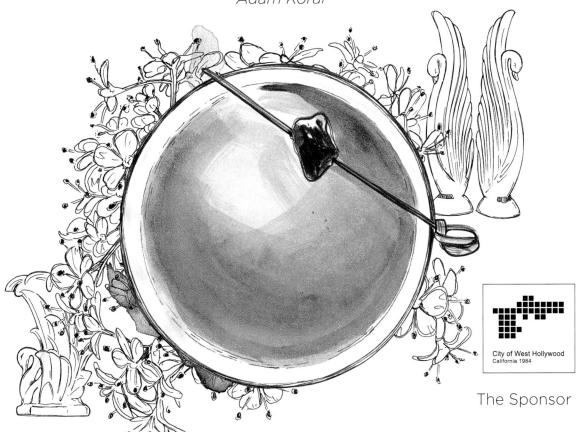

City of West Hollywood
California 1984

8288 Santa Monica Blvd.

The Nugget: Come as you are or whoever you want to be. You will never be excluded in this vibrant and inclusive place.

Hamburger Mary's has the legacy as America's first gay hamburger franchise. Mary's was born celebrating diversity as a dive beer and burger joint in 1972 San Francisco. Each city franchise is family owned and shows its own local flare.

In an article, Jewels, the director of entertainment and marketing, notes "It's not a gay bar." As Hamburger Mary's tagline suggests, it's a venue for everyone who wants to *Eat, Drink and be Mary.*

Hamburger Mary's has one of the best experiential Drag Queen Bingo nights. Drag Queen Bingo was invented by Judy Werle as part of AIDS Activism in the 1990s at Chicken Soup Brigade in Seattle, WA. Chicken Soup Brigade, now a program of Lifelong, has been feeding people affected by the virus and other terminal illnesses for over 40 years.

8288 Santa Monica Boulevard was built in 1956. Hamburger Mary's drag history is too fabulous and grand to mention. On occasion celebrities are known to perform at Mary's. In 2022, the *I Think We're Alone Now* icon, Tiffany, had a one-night-only show.

Bellini

The Mix:
3.5 oz Chandon Brut Sparkling Wine
1.5 oz Liquid Alchemist Peach Syrup

The Process:
Put the Liquid Alchemist Peach Syrup and Chandon Brut into
a champagne flute and stir a few times.

If you've visited Hamburger Mary's and took home one of their leg cups, lucky you!
Definitely make it in that. Multiply the recipe to fill this fabulous vessel.

The Creator:
Classic Italian Recipe

City of West Hollywood
California 1984

LIQUID ALCHEMIST
PREMIUM COCKTAIL SYRUPS

Hugo's
RESTAURANT

8401 Santa Monica Blvd.

The Nugget: Hugo's restaurant is a local neighborhood staple. If you can't think of where to go, you head to Hugo's. They never disappoint, catering to a variety of taste buds and dietary requirements.

Terry Kaplan and Rafael A. Nazario were the dynamic duo behind Hugo's famously extensive menu. Kaplan is a fifth-generation butcher, Word War II veteran, and a talented charcoal artist. Rafael A. Nazario is an accomplished musician whose classical compositions once provided background music at the restaurant.

In 1975, Kaplan purchased Hugo's specialty butcher, which had been at the location since the 1940s. Kaplan expanded and converted a space for dining next-door by knocking into the Monaco Grocery after they closed.

8401 Santa Monica Boulevard was built in 1927.

Bloody Mary or Michelada

The Boil:
Simple Syrup:
(Good for one month in the fridge, enough for one batch of Bloody Mary mix.)
Combine ¼ cup sugar with ¼ cup water in a pan and bring to a simmer.
Stir until the sugar is completely dissolved and then remove it from the heat.

The Wait:
Roasted Vegetables:
Put 1 red pepper, 4 roma tomatoes, and 1 ½ cloves garlic on a sheet pan.
Roast in a 350 °F oven for 40 minutes. Let cool.

The Prep:
Juice and fine strain 2 oz of lime juice (about two limes).
Juice and fine strain 1 ½ cups of lemon juice (about eight lemons).
Juice and fine strain 2 oz of orange juice (about one orange).
Juice and fine strain 4 oz of grapefruit juice (about half a grapefruit).

Sour Mix:
(Good for five days in fridge, enough for 1 ½ batches.)
Stir together ¼ cup simple syrup, the orange, grapefruit,
and lime juice with a ½ cup of the lemon juice and a pinch of salt.

Hugo's Bloody Mary Mix:
(Good for one week in the fridge, enough for sixteen cocktails.)
Blend roasted vegetables for two minutes. Add one 48 oz can of tomato juice, ¼ tsp garlic powder,
¼ tsp onion powder, 1 tbsp chipotle adobo paste, ½ tsp table salt, ⅛ tsp ground black pepper,
¼ oz horseradish root, and ½ tsp celery salt and blend for two more minutes.
Add 1 cup sour mix, 2 tbsp A-1 Steak Sauce, 1 tsp Tabasco, 1 tsp Cholula, and 1 cup lemon juice; mix well.

The Mix:
2 oz Tito's Vodka
Hugo's Bloody Mary Mix

The Process:
Fill a small hurricane glass with ice;
add vodka and bloody mix to fill.
Roll into a mixing tin and then back into the glass.

The Fandangle:
Garnish with a lime wedge,
celery stalk and skewered green olives.

VARIATION
The Michelada Mix:
2 oz Hugo's Bloody Mary Mix
1 can of Stone Buenaveza Salt & Lime Lager

The Process:
Pour half of the beer into a highball glass
that is half rimmed with tajin and filled with ice,
then add the Hugo's Bloody Mix.
Pour in the remaining beer as you are ready.

The Fandangle:
Garnish with a lime wedge and skewered green olives.

The Creator:
The Hugo's Team

City of West Hollywood
California 1984

Don't be a wallflower

La Bohème

8400 Santa Monica Blvd.

➡➤➤

The Nugget: 8400 Santa Monica Boulevard began life as the Paddock Pools in 1947. Followed by a mixed bag of businesses such as House of Pies, Posh Bagel, Matoi Restaurant, Iris Computer Store, Leo's Stereo, and in 1991, Café La Bohème. This café concept came from a chain in Japan and was the first in the USA. It was not however a nod to the infamous 1929-33 Café La Boheme on The Strip. The only thing the two venues have in common was the name—and a love of chandeliers.

The interior of Café La Bohème was created by the legendary restaurant designer, Margaret O'Brien. The original design even featured a small pool, a nod to the site's origins.

With resilience and the ability to adapt, the award-winning La Bohème (now minus the café) has been in business for 32 years and undergone multiple non-surgical facelifts. The most recent was to transform the parking lot into a magical outdoor dining space, a game-changer and life saver during the pandemic, and made La Bohème a more beloved space.

Maguey Picante

A.K.A. THE SITUATIONSHIP

The Boil:
Honey Pineapple Syrup:
(Good for two weeks in the fridge, enough for LOTS of cocktails!)
Peel and cube ¼ of a pineapple. In a saucepan, combine pineapple,
1 pinch of cinnamon, 1 whole clove, and 8 ¼ cups water.
Bring to a boil; reduce heat and simmer for 45 minutes, stirring occasionally.
Add ¾ cup honey and stir until it dissolves. Strain through a fine strainer.

The Prep:
Juice and fine strain one lime (enough for one cocktail).
Cut five cubes of fresh pineapple; each one less than 1" in size.

The Mix:
2 oz Dos Hombres Mezcal
.5 oz lime juice
1.5 oz honey pineapple syrup
5 cubes pineapple
5 dashes Hella Smoked Chili Bitters

The Process:
Muddle the pineapple cubes in a mixing tin. Add remaining ingredients and ice.
Shake and double strain into a chilled coupe glass that's half rimmed with agave worm salt.

The Creator:
Guido Ortuno, created for Aaron Paul and Bryan Cranston

DOS HOMBRES

Laurel HARDWARE
PLUMBING & ELECTRICAL SUPPLIES · KEYS · PAINT & GLASS

7984 Santa Monica Blvd.

The Nugget: Once a hardware store, always a hardware store; or is it? Don't be fooled by the Laurel Hardware sign out front. While it might be an ambiguous foible if you stumbled in looking for rope or duct tape, your discovery would be worth the misdirection. It's bigger on the inside! Interiors by Sam Marshall used reclaimed wood flooring salvaged from the 1934 Coney Island boardwalk; if those floors could talk, am I right! What would have been the stepping place for an order of ice-cream in Brooklyn is now your stomping ground for a west-coast, elevated cocktail from the Cole Apodaca menu.

7984 Santa Monica Boulevard was built in 1946. Research shows the first known occupant was called Reliable Hardware in 1958. By 1966, the name changed to Laurel Hardware. Laurel Hardware, the restaurant, opened in 2012.

L.A. Rosa

The Prep:
Juice and fine strain one lemon (enough for two cocktails).

The Mix:
2 oz Calirosa Rosa Blanco Tequila
.5 oz Ramazotti Rosato Aperitivo
.5 oz Giffard Strawberry Liqueur
.5 oz Liquid Alchemist Strawberry Syrup
.5 oz Liquid Alchemist Coconut Syrup
.75 oz lemon juice

The Process:
Shake all ingredients with ice and strain into a Collins glass over crushed ice.

The Fandangle:
Garnish with a pandan leaf and miniature red rose.

The Creator:
Cole Apodaca

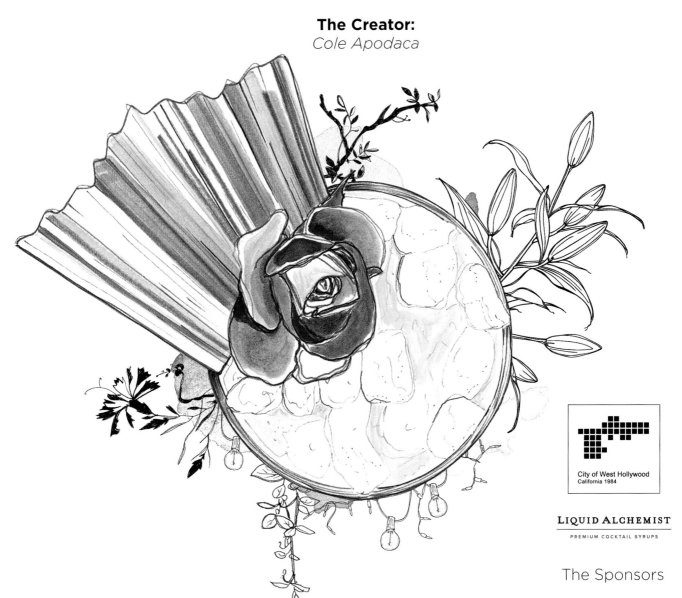

City of West Hollywood
California 1984

LIQUID ALCHEMIST
PREMIUM COCKTAIL SYRUPS

The Sponsors **96**

Norah

8279 Santa Monica Blvd.

The Nugget: "In any restaurant, true hospitality and a sense of welcome should always come first. I want to treat guests in my restaurants the way I treat people in my own home," explains Norah's owner, Rohan Talwar of IB Hospitality, in VoyageLA Magazine. "I wanted to create an unpretentious, inviting environment with high design and genuine warmth."

Norah is a local gem sitting behind an unmarked door with enough space inside to swing from its rafters. The interiors are designed by next-door-neighbor Thomas Schoos, who is no stranger to this property; the award-winning Schoos also designed the space for 8279 Santa Monica Boulevard's former tenant, O-bar.

The building was constructed in 1937 and has since been home to many, such as Jimmy Fly's Trap Café, Try Later Bar, Cheers, Al Capone's, Felt, O-bar, Don't Tell Mama, and Norah, which opened in 2016.

Blackbird

The Wait:
(Good for at least one month in fridge, makes enough for four cocktails.)
Thai Basil Gin:
Mix ½ cup loosely packed Thai basil leaves with 5 oz Bombay Sapphire gin.
Let sit for two days then fine strain (enough for four cocktails).

The Boil:
Blackberry Thai Basil Shrub:
(Good for two weeks in the fridge, enough for eightish cocktails.)
Heat 5 oz sugar, 5 oz water, 5 oz blackberries, and .25 oz Thai basil
in a pot until the blackberries are easily mashable.
Let sit for thirty minutes, then thoroughly mash blackberries with a potato masher.
Strain through a fine mesh strainer. Keep the blackberry/basil pulp for the next part of the recipe.

Blackberry Salt:
(Keep in a sealed container and store in a dry place; good for quite a while.)
Put the blackberry pulp onto a piece of parchment paper, then flatten evenly with a rolling pin.
Place the parchment paper on a sheet pan and bake at your oven's lowest setting; dehydrate until dry.
It should take at least eight hours. (You can use a dehydrator instead; if you're fancy!).
Freeze for at least two hours, then blend into a fine powder.
Mix the powder with an equal amount of sugar, half the amount of salt, and a pinch of citric acid.

The Prep:
Juice and fine strain one lime (enough for one cocktail).
Juice and fine strain one lemon (enough for six cocktails).

The Mix:
1.5 oz Thai basil-Infused Bombay Sapphire Dry Gin
.5 oz Strega Liqueur
1 oz blackberry Thai basil shrub
.5 oz lime juice
.25 oz lemon juice
1 oz brut cava

The Process:
Combine all ingredients except cava and shake with ice.
Strain into a rocks glass rimmed with Blackberry Salt and filled with fresh ice, top with cava.

The Fandangle:
Garnish with a skewered blackberry and a dehydrated lime wheel.

The Creator:
Rexx Cano

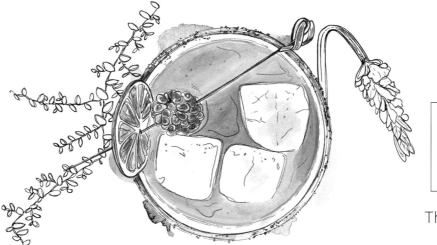

City of West Hollywood
California 1984

Send Noodz

phorage

7326 Santa Monica Blvd.

The Nugget: During Pride 2022, I couldn't stop watching an Instagram video featuring a cocktail with rainbow-colored sparkled salt. At our next Friday's R+D, I had us sipping-and-slipping up to the bar.

Phorage is one of *Once Upon a Cocktail's* 'diamonds in the rough,' located in a building complex behind a bank, it's the most unexpected place to find craft cocktails.

If you stop by this location check out the commissioned artwork by celebrated local artist Shplinton. The artist was asked to create three artworks related to cuisine and location of the restaurant. "One piece was the artist's interpretation of an iconic scene of Anthony Bourdain and Obama eating bun "vermicelli" in Hanoi... Another depicts the classic *Breakfast at Tiffany's* image of Audrey Hepburn, juxtaposed with two ladies smoking on the street during the Vietnam war. These artworks create a paradoxical social acceptance of one versus the other... and this otherness was what Shplinton was trying to evoke." Eric Cho, Phorage owner.

7326 Santa Monica Boulevard is somewhat void of a researchable history.

Pho-Mojito

The Wait:
Pho Infused Bacardí Superior Rum:
(Will keep indefinitely, enough for eight cocktails.)
In a pan over medium-high heat, toast one large cassia cinnamon stick,
one pod of cardamom (cracked), five pieces of star anise,
and five cloves until the spices become aromatic.
Add two cups of Bacardí Superior Rum.
Let mixture infuse in a cool, dry place for 24 hours, agitating occasionally, strain.

The Boil:
Lemongrass Simple Syrup:
(Good for one month in the fridge, enough for four cocktails.)
Combine ¼ cup sugar with ¼ cup water and half a stalk of chopped lemongrass, then bring to a simmer.
Stir until the sugar is completely dissolved then remove the pan from heat; fine strain.

The Prep:
Juice and fine strain one lime (enough for one cocktail).

The Mix:
2 oz pho-infused Bacardi Superior Rum
.75 oz lemongrass simple syrup
1 oz lime juice
4-5 mint leaves
2 Thai basil leaves
Q Mixers Club Soda

The Process:
Combine all ingredients, except soda water, in a mixing tin and shake with ice.
Dump without straining into a Collins glass filled with ice
and top with a small amount of the soda water.

The Fandangle:
Garnish with a lime wheel and a generous amount of Thai basil and mint.

The Creator:
Devon Espinosa

Q
MIXERS

City of West Hollywood
California 1984

SPEAKEASY

THE SURLY GOAT

7929 Santa Monica Blvd.

The Nugget: A quirky, mysterious dive bar is a rare unicorn in West Hollywood. As this book became more about drinking and experiences, it was imperative we represent bars who take pride in representing craft beer. Welcome to the Surly Goat.

The first restaurant to occupy the space was Alouette 1963, other venues to come and go were Figs, Belly Tapas Bar, a gay bar called iCandy Lounge, and a dance bar called Seven. The Surly Goat opened in 2009.

7929 Santa Monica Boulevard was built in two stages, the rear was constructed in 1912 and the front in 1950.

Craft Beer

The Prep:
To create your very own rotating selection of excellent craft beers at home,
go to your favorite craft beer shop.
The one that has rows and rows of different brands and styles of beer.
Now make your way to the local section and look for some that sound interesting.
Choose a few (try something new!) to stock your home fridge with.

The Wait:
If you're driving, you'll have to hold off on enjoying those beers until you get home.
Never drink and drive!

The Mix:
Craft Beer

The Process:
Pop the top, crack the can, or twist the top off your growler,
then gently pour the beer into a nice cold glass.

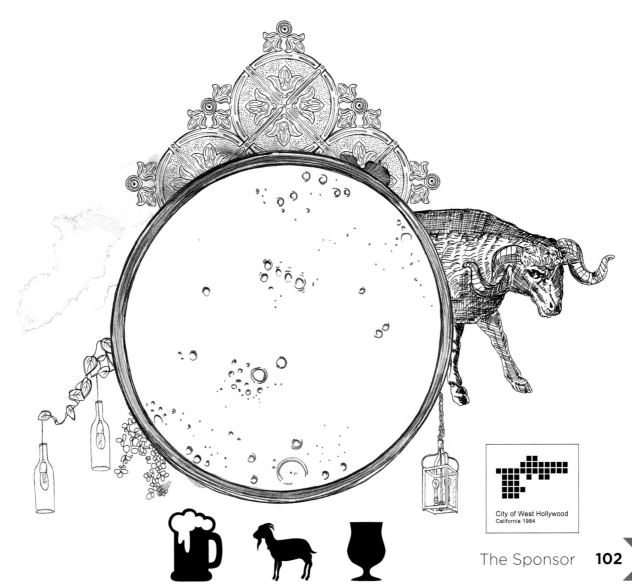

City of West Hollywood
California 1984

945 N Fairfax Ave.

The Nugget: Escorted through the white tunnel at Ysabel's entrance, you emerge in a paradise. A picturesque hideaway with dynamic seating options, the restaurant leaves you spoilt for choice. Whether at brunch, dusk, or an escapade in the twilight hours, Ysabel is a place of romantic dreams!

Twinkling lights wrap around olive trees in an atrium table-top setting, while the other restaurant space showcases a vintage supper club feel, where lovers can nuzzle in a booth. Salvaged marble, 100 years old repurposed from the Independence Hall in Philadelphia, covers bleacher-style seating near a fire pit, which is engulfed with loose, soft furnishings for added comfort. Throughout the entire restaurant, Ysabel's offers several nooks and crannies where one can steal a kiss, or two...

The 945 N Fairfax Avenue building was constructed in 1948. It has been home to restaurants such as Ma Maison, Hollywood Diner, Tutto Bene, Provencia, and a martini bar called Lola.

Ysabel Margarita

The Boil:
Agave Water:
(Good for one month in the fridge, enough for sixteen cocktails.)
Combine ½ cup agave syrup with ½ cup water and bring to a simmer.
Stir until agave syrup is completely dissolved and then remove from heat.

The Prep:
Juice and fine strain one lime (enough for one cocktail).

The Mix:
2 oz Cazadores Reposado Tequila
.5 oz agave water
1 oz lime juice
2 dashes orange bitters

The Process:
Combine all ingredients in a mixing tin with ice and shake.
Strain into a rocks glass filled with fresh ice.

The Fandangle:
Garnish with lime leaves.

The Creator:
By Cole Apodaca, based on a classic recipe.

City of West Hollywood
California 1984

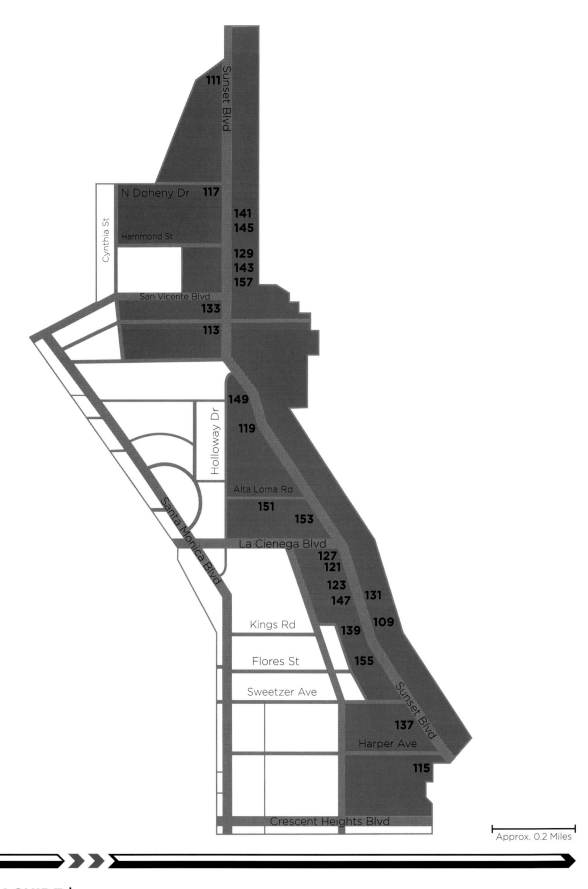

Approx. 0.2 Miles

MAP KEY GUIDE | The map number corresponds to venue location and the books page number.

Sunset Strip (SS) | Featuring Hans Fjellestad

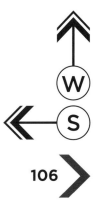

Hans Fjellestad

Sunset Strip is the muse behind countless songs, movies, dreams, stories, and it's been pulling people into its orbit for decades. With all that's happened here over the last 100+ years, I like to imagine the echoes are still reverberating and haunting the walls, the pavement, the air, just waiting for fellow travelers to tune into it.

There is some kind of magical, creative force behind this curvy mile-and-a-half stretch of road that's been around since it was a vital Tongva trade route, well before it evolved into the world's most famous nightclub scene in the 1920s or rock music's headquarters in the 1960s. Sunset Strip is a locus of constant reinvention, where each iteration leaves its mark.

Situated just outside the Los Angeles city limits–independent and wide open–The Strip was a place for letting go. During Hollywood's Golden Age, iconic hot spots like *Ciro's* (now *The Comedy Store*), the *Mocambo*, and the *Trocadero* drew the biggest entertainers of the day. It was a dizzying time of excess, mythmaking, seduction, and hedonism among the cultural elite. And that enigmatic castle on the hill, *Chateau Marmont**, helped keep their secrets. Like Columbia Pictures president, Harry Cohn, famously said, "If you must get into trouble, do it at the *Chateau Marmont**."

Few places expressed The Strip's unfettered heart at that time more than madam Lee Francis' bordello, *House of Francis* (now *Katana LA*), where misbehaving regulars like Clark Gable, Erroll Flynn, and Spencer Tracy were dragged out by studio fixers and Jean Harlow paid working girls and their clients to come home with her for gender-bending orgies. Wild times, if all the rumors are to be believed.

Of course, there remain many places on The Strip where you can commune with ghosts from the past. Like the *Rainbow Bar & Grill*–where the late Mötorhead frontman, Lemmy Kilmister, frequently sat drinking his Jack & Cokes in the same spot where Marilyn Monroe met Joe DiMaggio on a blind date decades earlier, when it was called *Villa Nova*. The Rainbow still carries on, relatively unchanged.

Sharing an alley with the Rainbow is *The Roxy Theatre*, which introduced us to the *Rocky Horror Show*, hosted John Lennon's "lost weekend," served John Belushi his last supper, launched entire genres of music, and remains a fixture of LA's music scene.

Continental Hyatt House, a few blocks down (now *Andaz West Hollywood*), is where Led Zeppelin and The Who raged and held court, and where Keith Richards famously threw a TV out his "Riot House" room window. You can still feel some of that crazy energy behind all the modern updates.

Across the street, Leland Bryant's 1929 LA Deco architectural icon, *Sunset Tower*, is the grand dame of West Hollywood. This is where Truman Capote penned In *Cold Blood*, Bugsy Siegel ran a gambling ring, Iggy Pop dove into the pool from his balcony, and Donna Summer wrote *Sunset People*. By the 1980s, *Sunset Tower* had become run down from neglect and was scheduled for demolition. Werner Klemperer (TV's Colonel Klink) refused eviction and stood his ground, even after the electricity and running water were shut off, until a law was passed that saved and preserved this precious landmark.

Other sites weren't so lucky and only live on in legend. At The Strip's east end was *Garden of Allah**–a bohemian paradise created by silent movie star Alla Nazimova–where Greta Garbo, Buster Keaton, F. Scott Fitzgerald, Harpo Marx, Ava Gardner, Humphrey Bogart, Dorothy Parker, Ernest Hemingway, John Barrymore, Joe Lewis, Cole Porter, Marlene Dietrich, and Laurence Olivier all lived in bungalows at one time or another in a tangle of phony marriages, fist-fights, booze, sex, and drugs. One writer called the Garden's inhabitants "a fast-living, hard-drinking, high-rolling lot who burned out fast and took the Garden with them."

The Garden might not be around anymore, but next door you can raise a glass at *The DEN on Sunset*, formerly the *Fifth Estate* coffee house, the epicenter of the 1966 Teen Riots, and where Art Kunkin and his young crew were in the basement, beavering away on America's first, and largest, alternative weekly newspaper, the *Freep* (LA Free Press).

So much history, so many stories. There's truly no place quite like Sunset Strip. It may have lost some of its luster over the decades, but rest assured, it remains a singular locale to gather and pour one out for the past and toast the future… maybe over a *Moscow Mule* (born on the Strip in 1941).

〉〉

Hans Fjellestad is a documentary filmmaker, musician, and educator in Los Angeles. Hans helmed the feature documentary Sunset Strip, which tracks the century-long history of the legendary street. The film premiered at SXSW, was released theatrically in 2012, and broadcast on Showtime.

hansfjellestad.com

*While these historical venues are geographically just outside West Hollywood's borders, they are an integral part of the story that made this 1.5 miles stretch of Sunset Boulevard famously known as The Sunset Strip.

ANDAZ. | WEST HOLLYWOOD
LOS ANGELES

8401 Sunset Blvd.

The Nugget: There is a difference between acknowledging the past and being held hostage to it. Andaz, with their contemporary renovations, pays homage but also breaks free from a time in history when it was known for the chaos and debauchery that shaped its identity and earned the nickname Riot Hyatt.

The legendary song *Whole Lotta Love* was already a few years old when, on tour, Led Zeppelin's entourage occupied the sixth floor in this hotel. During their stay, John Bonham famously rode a motorcycle through the corridor and both Keith's, Richards and Moon, threw TV's from high rise windows.

In 1984, the mockumentary *This is Spinal Tap* filmed their end-of-tour party on the roof. And in full life cycle (life imitating art), scenes from Cameron Crow's 2000 film, *Almost Famous*, were shot onsite with refurbished décor to match the original 1970s design. In 2022, Amazon's, *Daisy Jones & the Six* repeated Crow's history and took over the venue for a modern adaptation and homage to "unnamed" infamous rock band from the '70s.

These antics held a whole-lot-of-love for decades—five of them. Through it all, the Andaz proves to honor all music: past, present, and future.

Paradise City

The Wait:
Coconut Infused Casamigos Reposado:
(Good for at least one month in the fridge, enough for eleven cocktails.)
Mix one 750 ml bottle of Casamigos Reposado with ½ cup toasted,
unsweetened coconut flakes. Place the infusion in the fridge, agitating it 1x/day.
After two weeks, pour it through a fine strainer and then through a coffee filter.

The Boil:
Cinnamon Syrup:
(Good for one month in the fridge, enough for eight cocktails.)
Put one roughly broken up cinnamon stick in a sauce pan and toast over medium heat.
When the cinnamon becomes aromatic (about two minutes)
add 5 oz of water and 1 cup of raw sugar.
Increase heat to high and bring to a boil while stirring occasionally.
Remove from heat when sugar is dissolved.
Once mixture is cooled, pour through a fine mesh strainer.

The Prep:
Juice and fine strain one lime (enough for one cocktail).
Juice and fine strain ¼ of a pineapple (enough for ten cocktails).
Crush ice; a Lewis bag and a heavy muddler work great for this.

The Mix:
2 oz coconut-infused Casamigos Reposado Tequila
.75 oz cinnamon syrup
.75 oz fresh pineapple juice
.75 oz lime juice
1 dash Angostura Bitters

The Process:
Shake all ingredients with ice in a cocktail shaker.
Pour over crushed ice into a tropical-style glass.

The Fandangle:
Two pineapple fronds, a rosemary sprig, and a torched cinnamon stick.

The Creator:
Emilio Lourdes

CASAMIGOS
Tequila

West
Hollywood

BOA
Steakhouse

9200 Sunset Blvd.

➤➤➤➤

The Nugget: "I am firm in my belief that architecture is a business and not an art," Charles Luckman once told a writer for *The New Yorker*.

Ironically, Luckman achieved both, designing the iconic Theme Building at LAX and The Forum in Inglewood. Luckman conceived 9200 Sunset Tower (not to be confused with the hotel) as a commercial enterprise in 1971. Originally called Luckman Tower, then Luckman Plaza, the structure today is known as 9200 Sunset Boulevard, and the home of BOA Steakhouse.

At one time, Luckman Plaza was home to a notorious private investigator who wouldn't open a case without a $25,000 retainer. During a raid in 2002, the FBI uncovered an elaborate and illegal wiretapping system, which targeted the rich and famous, and a safe containing hand grenades and C-4 explosives. Luckily the raid occurred before the PI could set his explosives. Disaster avoided!

A year earlier, BOA first opened its doors at 8462, the former Grafton (now Hotel Ziggy, SS | 123). In 2009, after 9200 Sunset Boulevard's multimillion-dollar overhaul, BOA moved into their new, expansive restaurant space.

Bee Blossom

The Wait:
Honey Ice Pop:
We recommend using a cocktail ice tray that makes 1.25" cubes.
Fill each compartment of an ice cube tray with ¼ oz honey syrup, ¾ oz water
(use the same measurements if you're using a standard ice cube tray),
and a small wooden honey dipper stick, then freeze.

The Boil:
Honey Syrup:
(Good for one month in the fridge, enough for roughly four cocktails.)
Combine ½ cup California wildflower honey with ½ cup water and bring to a simmer.
Stir until honey is completely dissolved, then remove from heat.

The Prep:
Juice and fine strain one lemon (enough for two cocktails).

The Mix:
2 oz Roku Gin
1 oz California wildflower honey syrup
.5 oz lemon juice
1 egg white*

The Process:
Combine all ingredients in a mixing tin and shake without ice. Add ice, shake again,
then strain into a honeypot glass (or a rocks glass) over fresh ice.

The Fandangle:
Garnish with an edible marigold and a honey ice pop.

The Creator:
Tara Shadzi

Beam SUNTORY

ROKU GIN
THE JAPANESE CRAFT GIN

*Consuming raw eggs may increase your risk of foodborne illness, which can be especially dangerous if you have certain medical conditions, such as pregnancy.

8830 Sunset Blvd.

The Nugget: "Swing along with our lovely uninhibited dancers," announced a classified ad in the July 1966 LA Times for The Classic Cat, which aimed to coax visitors to where the action was, whether they sought a cozy interlude with a date, its plush décor, or to simply enjoy girl-watching, "the Classic Cat is for YOU!" the ad boasted.

The 1965 club's original entrance was on the southeast corner of Sunset and Larrabee. Upon the building's façade sat signage that was updated over the decades, changing to accommodate each new business inhabiting the space-the Jerry Lewis Restaurant, Le Parisian, University Stereo, Tower Video, and Chase Bank.

Today, The Classic Cat honors its namesake while embodying the historical, ethereal spirit of the venue with a night to remember.

Burlesque Fuse

The Boil:
Simple Syrup:
(Good for one month in fridge, enough for ten cocktails.)
Combine ½ cup sugar with ½ cup water and bring to a simmer;
stir until the sugar is completely dissolved, then remove pan from heat.

The Prep:
Juice and fine strain one lemon (enough for two cocktails).

The Mix:
1.5 oz Neft Vodka
.75 oz Aperol Aperitivo
.5 oz lemon juice
.5 oz simple syrup
1 dash Bittermens Burlesque Bitters
1 drop orange blossom water
prosecco

The Process:
Shake all ingredients, except prosecco, with ice and strain over a wine glass filled with ice.
Top with the prosecco.

The Fandangle:
Fresh blueberries and raspberries.

The Creator:
Stephanie Delgado

NEFT
VODKA

8226 Sunset Blvd.

▶▶▶

The Nugget: This building's 1964 tenants were the Fifth Estate coffee house, an art gallery, and a radical literature lending library. The basement housed a printing press where the *Freep* (LA Free Press) took up residency. This press was used to print protest flyers for The Sunset Strip Riots. These "Youth Riots" were a revolt against imposed curfews, an infringement of civil liberties, and the right to gather in public. The tensions and protests swelled for weeks. The conflict climaxed on Saturday, November 12, 1966, a historical night on The Strip, which led to several weeks of unrest.

The Coffee House plaque on the building's façade is a nod to the 1999-2003 tenant that was featured on a season 3 episode of *Sex in the City*, "Sex and Another City."

The space has had multiple facelifts over the years, the most extreme being from a waffle house to a naked sushi restaurant! For the past fourteen years, it has been beloved as The DEN on Sunset. The building celebrated its centennial in 2023.

Spicy Paloma

The Wait:
Spicy Cazadores Blanco Tequila:
(Good for one month in the fridge, enough for five cocktails.)
To make spicy tequila, slice two serrano peppers and soak in 12 oz of Cazadores Blanco
in a covered container for 24 hours. Fine strain.

The Boil:
Cocktail Agave Syrup:
(Good for one month in the fridge, enough for eight cocktails.)
Combine ½ cup agave syrup with ¼ cup water and bring to a simmer.
Stir until agave syrup is completely dissolved and then remove from heat.

The Prep:
Juice and fine strain one lime (enough for one cocktail).
Juice and fine strain half a grapefruit (enough for three cocktails).

The Mix:
2 oz spicy Cazadores Blanco Tequila
.75 oz cocktail agave syrup
1 oz grapefruit juice
.5 oz lime juice
soda water
.5 oz El Silencio Espadín Mezcal

The Process:
Combine all ingredients except soda and mezcal in a mixing tin and shake with ice.
Strain into a Collins glass filled with fresh ice. Top with soda water and give it a gentle stir.

The Fandangle:
Float the .5 oz of El Silencio on top of the Paloma,
then garnish with a dusting of paprika salt and a lime wedge.

The Creator:
Shawn Ilardi and John Jordan

Q
MIXERS

MEZCAL
El Silencio

THE
SUNSET
STRIP

The Sponsors 116 >

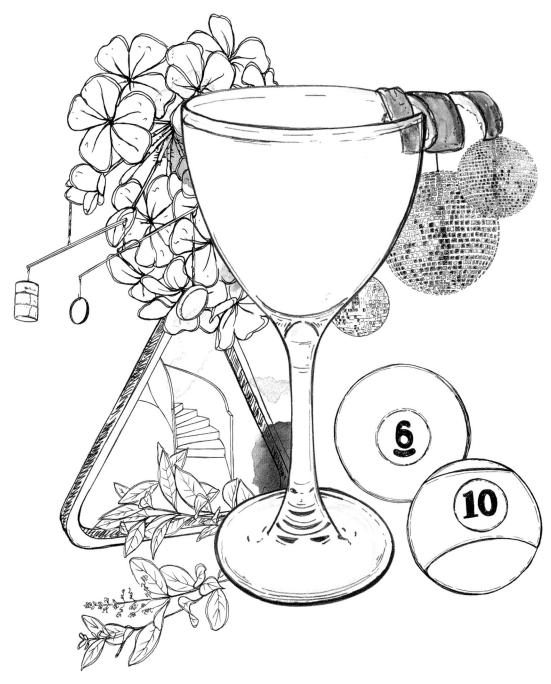

9040 Sunset Blvd.

The Nugget: Edward Fickett, a celebrated California architect and onetime architectural advisor to President Eisenhower, designed the original building at 9040 Sunset Boulevard in 1947, which was demolished to make way for The West Hollywood EDITION built in 2019.

Sometimes we melt gold to make way for a contemporary treasure. The Fickett building, a nugget in WeHo history, housed a restaurant named Scandia, which opened in 1957. The exclusive Scandinavian and French cuisine eatery was also the Rat Pack's headquarters. Frank Sinatra kept an office upstairs, complete with a personal shower. The original restaurant owners, Ken and Tova Hensen, sold the business in the 1970s and it closed for good in 1989. Other concepts came and went until Ian Schrager's progressive development was green lit.

This illustrious new hotel is designed by the father of modern architectural minimalism, John Pawson, CBE,— in his own right, an honorable legend like Fickett! Pawson describes the character of West Hollywood as "the way glamor and grittiness have historically rubbed up against one another." This intriguing observation shows in the hotel's design direction.

Lost in Tarzana

The Boil:
Cocktail Agave Syrup:
(Good for one month in the fridge, enough for 24 cocktails.)
Combine ½ cup agave syrup with ¼ cup water and bring to a simmer.
Stir until agave syrup is completely dissolved and then remove from heat.

The Prep:
Juice and fine strain half a lemon (enough for three cocktails).

The Mix:
2 oz Del Maguey Vida Mezcal
.25 oz Chareau Aloe Liqueur
.25 oz Cocchi Americano Aromatized Wine
.25 oz cocktail agave syrup
.25 oz lemon juice
2 dashes orange bitters

The Process:
Combine all ingredients in a mixing tin and shake with ice.
Strain into a Nick and Nora glass.

The Fandangle:
Garnish with a lime twist.

The Creator:
Michael Krajcar

West
Hollywood

eveleigh

8752 Sunset Blvd.

➤➤➤

The Nugget: This building was a private residence in 1930. By the 1960s, it was being used as a commercial space. Renovations to create additional office spaces for Kragen & Company took place in 1980. It was Kenneth Kragen, of Kragen & Company, who spearheaded the 1985 Live Aid USA for Africa concert, the project that gave us the hit single, "We Are the World." Another former 8752 Sunset Boulevard occupant was a Kenneth Cole Shoe store, which had its own mini-Walk of Fame. The footprints outside the shop featured celebrities such as Elizabeth Taylor and Richard Gere. With time the footprints vanished, unlike the Eveleigh cocktail Sibling Warfare. This herbaceous and spicy profile leaves a lasting impression.

Sibling Warfare

The Wait:
Basil Syrup:
(Good for two weeks in the fridge, enough for four cocktails.)
Thoroughly blend .25 oz of packed basil leaves, ¾ tsp of fresh peeled sliced ginger,
two thin slices of jalapeño, 3 oz simple syrup, and a tiny pinch of salt.
Let sit for a few minutes then skim off the top layer of film before bottling.

The Boil:
Simple Syrup:
(Good for one month in the fridge, enough for one batch of basil syrup.)
Combine ½ cup sugar with ½ cup water and bring to a simmer;
stir until the sugar is completely dissolved and then remove the pan from heat.

The Prep:
Juice and fine strain one lime (enough for one cocktail).

The Mix:
1 oz mezcal
1 oz blanco tequila
.75 oz basil syrup
1 oz lime juice

The Process:
Combine all ingredients in a mixing tin and shake with ice. Double strain into a coupe.

The Fandangle:
Garnish with a lime wheel.

The Creator:
Johnny Uhorchuk

THE
**SUNSET
STRIP**

DAVE'S CORNER

HARRIET'S

8490 Sunset Blvd.

The Nugget: When Jack climbed the beanstalk, he found the golden goose. The h.wood Group is notorious for creating exquisite, golden-egg venues. Harriet's is another powerhouse for the Group, perched in the sky and located on the rooftop of the 1 Hotel.

Harriet's is a wonderous outdoor-indoor space to sip away on The Skyline cocktail, made with Kuleana Rum Agricole, from the first-ever distillery on the Big Island of Hawaii.

Fee, Fi, Fo Rum, will have you climbing the sugarcane (ok so there are elevators), time and time again!

Skyline

The Prep:
Ginger Syrup:
(Good for two weeks in the fridge, enough for sixteen cocktails.)
Peel and chop an 8 oz piece of ginger. Run ginger through a juicer;
(if you have to use a blender add just enough water for the ginger to blend).
strain the juice and combine with the amount of sugar equal to the liquid output
(for example if you get 4 oz of ginger juice you would use 4 oz of sugar).
Stir or shake until the sugar is thoroughly dissolved.

Fresh Raspberry Syrup:
(Good for two weeks in the fridge, enough for sixteen cocktails.)
Juice and fine strain about one 6 oz container of raspberries, enough to get 5 oz of juice;
combine with 5 oz of sugar and stir or shake until the sugar is dissolved.

Juice and fine strain one lime (enough for one cocktail).

The Mix:
2 oz Kuleana Hawaiian Agricole Rum
.5 oz ginger syrup
.5 oz raspberry syrup
1 oz lime juice
1 dash Regan's Orange Bitters
club soda

The Process:
Combine all ingredients, except soda water, in a mixing tin and shake with ice.
Strain into a Collins glass over ice, top with club soda.

The Fandangle:
Garnish with a lime wedge.

The Creator:
Josh Goldman

KULEANA
RUM WORKS

THE
SUNSET
STRIP

Bitch DONT KILL MY Vibe

HOTEL ZIGGY

8462 Sunset Blvd.

⟩⟩

The Nugget: In a 1977 CBC News interview, David Bowie comments on his titular alter ego Ziggy Stardust, "I wanted to define the archetype messiah rock star using the trappings of Kabuki theater, mime technique, fringe New York music. My references were the Velvet Underground, and a British view of American Street energy."

Bowie-influences and the spirit of Ziggy vibrate through the hotel with the addition of awe-inspiring murals by CJ Hungerman. I'd suggest sitting amongst the artwork poolside while sipping on your Witchy Woman cocktail. The drink references the eponymous song by The Eagles, 1972. Don Henley penned the lyrics, which drew inspiration from both the 1970s "white witchcraft" trend and Zelda Fitzgerald's biography. Zelda, like Bowie, is an icon of freedom. Zelda was also an on-and-off again WeHo resident with her husband, Mr. Golden Age himself, _The Great Gatsby_ author, F. Scott Fitzgerald.

The building was constructed in 1955 as the Park Sunset Apartments and converted into the Grafton Hotel in 2000 (also the original home of BOA Steakhouse 2001, SS | 111).

With a huge fire cracking explosion of electric stardust, Hotel Ziggy opened in 2022.

Witchy Woman

The Prep:
Juice and fine strain one lime (enough for one cocktail).
Carefully peel one prickly pear, holding the fruit with a towel to avoid its barbs.
Cut into cubes and purée in a blender (enough for two cocktails).

The Mix:
1.5 oz Casamigos Reposado Tequila
.5 oz Cointreau Orange Liqueur
.75 oz prickly pear purée
.75 oz lime juice

The Process:
Shake all ingredients in a shaker tin with ice.
Strain into a rocks glass filled with ice, half rimmed with black salt.

The Fandangle:
Garnish with a wheel of dehydrated lime and orange.

The Creator:
Tobin Salas

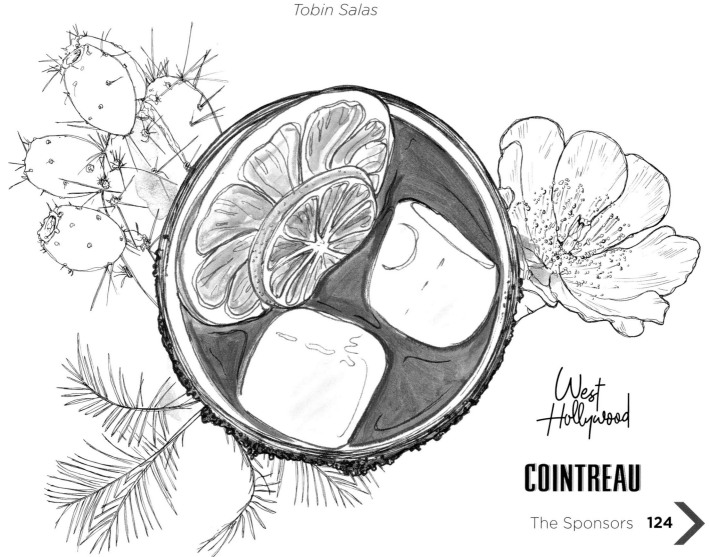

West
Hollywood

COINTREAU

HOTEL ✴ ZIGGY

8462 Sunset Blvd.

The Nugget: On the morning of August 12, I was up early to bake. I arrived at Hotel Ziggy for R+D with Sarah and a treat in hand. After some nibbles, the hotel team loved my concept and bought the recipe. Voilà; welcome to Jameson Orange Sticky Toffee Pudding!

The origins of sticky toffee pudding are highly disputed, with bakers in the north of Britain and Canada staking claims. Either way, the first published recipe was in 1971.

With Hotel Ziggy's recipe, I brought it back to the USA with a more banana-bread feel (its recipe was first published stateside in 1933). Hotel Ziggy's is now served with a hybrid of origins that Ancesty.com would relish featuring flavors from North America, Britain, Canada, and Ireland.

Jameson Orange Sticky Toffee Pudding

(The recipe makes approx. four 5 oz servings.)

The Mix:
Jameson pudding: using the gram scale
½ cup 1 ¼ tsp (120g) golden brown sugar
½ cup 1 ¼ tsp (120g) unsalted butter
½ cup 1 ¼ tsp (120g) all-purpose flour
1 ¾ tsp (8g) baking powder
½ cup peeled chopped ripe banana (approx. 1 banana)
2 tbsp pitted dried dates (approx. 5) finely chopped or use a Magic Bullet (if you are lucky to have one)
1 egg
2 oz of Jameson Orange Irish Whiskey

The Prep:
Preheat the oven to 350° Fahrenheit.
In a mixing bowl, cream the butter and sugar with a electric-hand-whisk.
Whisk in the egg, and Jameson Orange.
Chop the banana into pieces. Hand chop, or Magic Bullet, the dates. Whip the banana and dates into the mixture.
Fold in the flour and baking powder until fully incorporated and the batter has a fluffy consistency.
Release-Spray (chef's secret) four, single 6 oz baking ramekins.
With a pen, trace around the bottom of your mold onto parchment paper, cut out the circle about
⅛ of an inch inside the line, Spray-Release the paper and add to the inside the ramekin.
Using a scale, measure 5 oz of the batter into each ramekin (allowing room for proofing).

The Wait:
Place all four ramekins onto a baking sheet and bake in the center of the oven for thirty minutes–then check
the middle of the pudding with skewer, if the skewer pulls out clean-we're cooked.
If the skewer isn't clean, close the door and check again in two minute increments until the skewer comes out clean.
Allow the pudding to rest for a few minutes before carefully releasing it from the mold.
Remove the parchment paper and place on a cooling rack for ten minutes.
The cool air will make the sides crust, which becomes delightfully gooey when the toffee sauce is added.

The Mix:
Jameson Toffee Sauce:
¼ cup (60g) golden brown sugar
¼ cup (60g) unsalted butter
⅓ cup 1 ¼ tsp (90g) Lyles Golden Syrup
½ cup or 120 ml whipping cream
1.5 oz of Jameson Orange

The Prep: 45 minutes:
Three-15 minute stages
1) In a saucepan over low-heat, dissolve the sugar and butter in the Golden Syrup, stirring constantly for fifteen minutes.
2) Slowly add the cream, stirring until it's back to a slow simmer over low heat (do not allow it to over boil).
3) Still over low heat, stir the Jameson Orange into the toffee sauce for approximately fifteen minutes,
simmering until mixture reaches toffee-sauce consistency.

The Process:
Pour the hot Jameson toffee sauce over the hot pudding.

The Fandangle:
Serve with a pillow of whipped cream and a dehydrated orange wheel.
Eat! Eat some more, or share with a friend, if you're in a sharing kinda mood.

The Creator:
Chef Gabriel Contreras and Katie Brightside

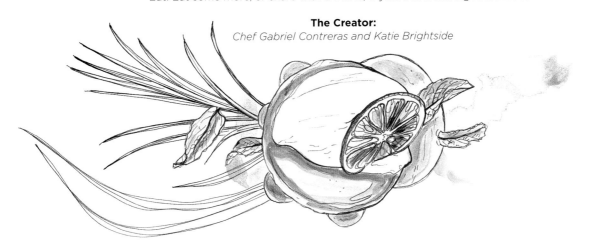

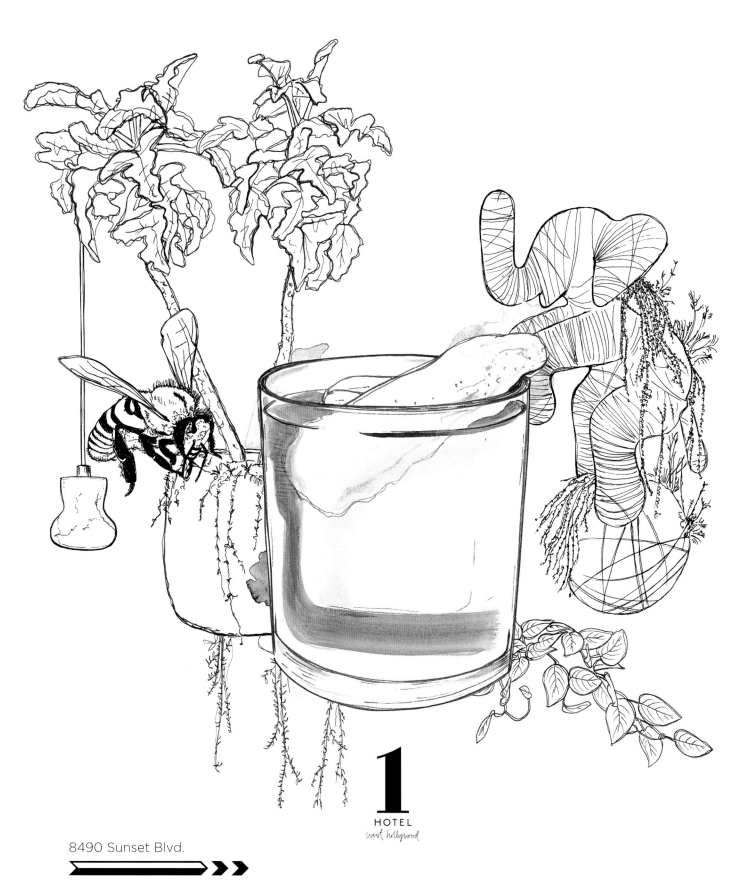

1
HOTEL
west hollywood

8490 Sunset Blvd.

The Nugget: Since 2017, the 1 Hotel has had a few previous iterations including The Jeremy and The James. The Dream Catcher installation that integrates between the architecture of the two towers of the 1 Hotel is one of the largest public sculptures in West Hollywood. By artist Janet Echelman, it is a visual response to her research on brainwaves during dream periods. The positioning of the piece within the epicenter of The Strip lends a purposeful nod to Los Angeles' pursuit of dreams.

Prior to the 1 Hotel, in 1964, a seven-story building designed by architect Daniel L. Dworsky sat on the land. In 1967 it was acquired by Petersen Publishing to house numerous publications such as *Hot Rod Magazine* devoted to drag racing, muscle cars, and hot rodding–the same Petersen who founded the Petersen Automotive Museum on Miracle Mile.

Eagle Rocked

The Prep:
5% Saline Solution:
(Will keep indefinitely, enough for lots of cocktails.)
Mix 100 grams (about 3.5 oz) of water
with 5 grams (about ¾ tsp) of kosher salt until the salt is dissolved.

The Mix:
2 oz Calirosa Añejo Tequila
1 oz Bigallet China China Liqueur
.5 oz Montenegro Amaro
2 dashes Fee Brothers Aztec Chocolate Bitters
3 drops saline solution

The Process:
Combine all ingredients in a mixing glass and stir with ice.
Strain into a rocks glass over a big ice cube.

The Fandangle:
Garnish with a burnt orange peel.

The Creator:
Steven Minor

West Hollywood

We've been so busy keepin' up with the Jones'... Maybe it's time we got back to the basics of love

8917 Sunset Blvd.

The Nugget: After construction finished in 1937, the space opened as Little Hungary, which advertised Hungarian food and Romani music. From 1941 to 1947, it housed the Little Gypsy.* Archival images suggest the restaurant had a sensational façade and decorative awning.

Rose Deitch took the helm for a decade with three different concepts starting in 1960 with The Golden Violin. The Clan opened in 1963 and was billed as Sunset Strip's most intimate supper club. In 1964 it switcheroo'ed to The Galaxy Dance, which was wedged in the thick of The Sunset Strip Riots. It was such a successful club, Rose opened a second space next door, The Galaxy Overflow, where Rock & Reilly's is now (SS | 143).

After the Galaxy tenure came Thelma, which hosted performances from Ike and Tina Turner's 1969 tour and the Grateful Dead's only LA appearances that year.

Later, five separately operated Sushi concepts and restaurant Gorge filled the space. Then in spring 2021, 8917 Sunset Boulevard birthed us Justin Queso's Tex-Mex—JQ Ranch Water please!

*Use of some terms are historical.

TX's Ranch Water

The Prep:
Juice and fine strain one lime (enough for one cocktail).

The Mix:
2 oz blanco tequila
1 oz lime juice
4 oz Topo Chico Mineral Water

The Process:
Combine all ingredients in a pint glass filled with ice.
Roll into a shaker tin then strain into a 16 oz glass half rimmed with tajin
and filled with fresh ice.

The Fandangle:
Garnish with a lime wedge.

The Creator:
*This modern classic was chosen for the bar's cocktail menu
by opening bar manager, Greig Borthwick.*

THE
**SUNSET
STRIP**

KATANA
robata and sushi bar

8439 Sunset Blvd.

The Nugget: Designed by architect Charles Sherman Cobb, in a Renaissance Revival style, 8439 Sunset Boulevard had one of the most scandalous lives of The Strip buildings.

The Piazza del Sol has changed its name more times than rock royalty, Prince. It was formerly known in 1927 as Hacienda Park Apartments and as the Coronet Apartments in 1939. After an arson attack that burned the building to its shell, a 1985 restoration repurposed the space as an office building.

Its most sensationalistic period was in the 1930s, when a Hollywood Madam, Lee Francis, ran an A-List bordello—Ooh La La! In her 1965 memoir, *Ladies on Call*, Francis claimed that Jean Harlow was a frequent guest and would often drop by to take on a customer for herself.

In a January 2002 LA Times article on Katana, Merrill Shindler quipped, "[t]hese guys will do great, they can live for five years on the buzz alone." Twenty years later Katana is more than just a hum!

Tropical Hibiscus

The Wait:
Hibiscus Tea Infused Dahlia Cristalino Tequila:
(Good in the fridge for two weeks, enough for four cocktails.)
Put one hibiscus tea bag into 6 oz of Dahlia Cristalino;
let sit for two hours and then remove tea bag.

The Prep:
Juice and fine strain one lime (enough for one cocktail).

The Mix:
1.5 oz hibiscus tea-infused Dahlia Cristalino Tequila
.5 oz Giffard Passion Fruit Liqueur
.5 oz Liquid Alchemist Coconut Syrup
.5 oz lime juice

The Process:
Combine all ingredients in a mixing tin and shake with ice.
Strain into a rocks glass filled with fresh ice.

The Fandangle:
Top with a float of pomegranate juice then garnish
with three edible firesticks and a fresh edible hibiscus flower.

The Creator:
Jasmine Garcia

TEQUILA
DAHLIA®
CRISTALINO

LIQUID ALCHEMIST
PREMIUM COCKTAIL SYRUPS

THE
L O N D O N
WEST HOLLYWOOD

1020 N San Vicente Blvd.

The Nugget: 1984 was the year the City of West Hollywood became an independent incorporated city. It was also the year that hairbands descended onto The Strip. Another newcomer in town, situated only a stone's throw away, was Le Bel Age Hotel, a five-star opulent hotel which featured two restaurants. Diaghilev, with its romantic interior, evoked 1920s Russia with French-inspired Russian cuisine. La Brasserie, with old Hollywood décor, was a restaurant-turned jazz venue on the weekends called Club Brasserie, that pulled from the talented local players on the LA jazz scene.

In October 1990, Darren Star and Aaron Spelling's *Beverly Hills, 90210* hit our tv screen with many scenes filmed on location at the Bel Age Hotel (now minus the Le!). While the infamous show ricocheted across the planet, highlighting the dramas of wealthy teens, the music on Sunset switcheroroo'ed again, drawing more and more contrast between the mainstream and its apathetic counterculture.

Panoma 94

The Boil:
Simple Syrup:
(Good for one month in the fridge, enough for five cocktails.)
Combine ¼ cup sugar with ¼ cup water and bring to a simmer;
stir until the sugar is completely dissolved and then remove the pan from heat.

The Prep:
Juice and fine strain half a grapefruit (enough for four cocktails).
Juice and fine strain one lime (enough for two cocktails).

The Mix:
2 oz Seedlip Spice 94 Non-Alcoholic Spirit
.5 oz simple syrup
1 oz grapefruit juice
.5 oz lime juice
soda water

The Process:
Lightly shake all ingredients with ice. Strain into a highball glass filled with ice.

The Fandangle:
Garnish with a lime wheel.

The Creator:
Dave Whitton

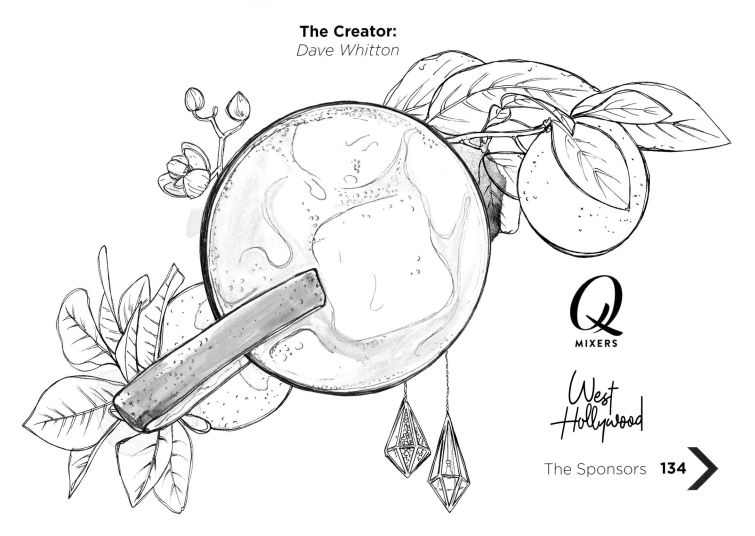

Q MIXERS

West Hollywood

THE
LONDON
WEST HOLLYWOOD

1020 N San Vicente Blvd.

The Nugget: In 2008, The London West Hollywood at Beverly Hills—with no shortage of swank—opened its doors with a glassed-in rooftop pool. Possessing a villa in the sky, The London has one of the largest penthouses featuring 360 degree views of the City of Los Angeles. Dame Vivienne Westwood (R.I.P.) and British architecture and design firm, David Collins Studio, custom designed the interiors of the penthouse, eliminating the '80s décor!

2008 was the year that started the Annual Sunset Strip Festival, which had an incredible seven-year run. Bands such as Ozzy Osbourne, Ace Frehley, Jane's Addiction, Mötley Crüe, LA Guns, Linkin Park, Empire of the Sun, Smashing Pumpkins, and Kid Cudi performed.

Nikko Niigata

The Boil:
Honey Syrup:
(Good for one month in the fridge, enough for 24 cocktails.)
Combine ½ cup honey with ¼ cup water and bring to a simmer.
Stir until the honey is completely dissolved and then remove from heat.

The Prep:
Juice and fine strain one lemon (enough for one cocktail).
Juice and fine strain ¼ of a pineapple (enough for eight cocktails).

The Mix:
2 oz Shibui Grain Select Japanese Whisky
.5 oz Liquid Alchemist Passion Fruit Syrup
.25 oz honey syrup
1 oz pineapple juice
.75 oz lemon juice

The Process:
Combine all ingredients in a mixing tin and shake with ice.
Strain into a rocks glass over a big cube.

The Fandangle:
Garnish with a pineapple frond and lemon zest.

The Creator:
Dave Whitton

West Hollywood

LIQUID ALCHEMIST
PREMIUM COCKTAIL SYRUPS

8264 Sunset Blvd.

The Nugget: The mural on the westside wall of the building illustrates an arrow pointing to the entrance of the Naughty Pig, proclaiming, *Good Times Here!* It does exactly what it says on the tin! Want to let your hair down, and paint the town pig? Walk on in!

The structure was originally built in 1924 as a private residence and was renovated in 1945. The first restaurant in the space, The Players Choice, opened in 1967 and served "snazzy soul food". In 1970, it converted into Knowpow's Comedy Room hosting two shows a night. The next occupant, Left Bank restaurant, relocated after a building fire. A fresh renovation in 1975 brought the British pub-themed Copperfield's Inn, followed by Mika Sushi, Sushi on Sunset, Empress, and the '80s inspired Lazer Kat. The latter's interiors still haunt The Pig with feline restroom art.

Vodka Soda

The Wait:
Perhaps take some time to think about Kástra Elion?
It's a unique vodka that's made with olives!
Owned by West Hollywood locals and produced in Greece in the owner's ancestral town.

The Mix:
1.5 oz Kástra Elión (or maybe more…)
soda water

The Process:
Fill a bucket glass with ice, pour in the vodka, and then add soda water.
Give it a little stir so the vodka and the soda become one.

The Fandangle:
Garnish with a lime wedge.

Shitters

THE
SUNSET
STRIP

PENDRY
WEST HOLLYWOOD

8430 Sunset Blvd.

The Nugget: If only we could make the past and present coexist at 8430 Sunset Boulevard. But change is good and history is a sum of the events, people, and tangible things that lead you to now. Nostalgia reminds us that the John Barrymore estate (Drew's grandfather) would have been a glorious site to visit. The estate sprawled across the corner of Olive and Sunset.

If there was a time portal, you could go back and swig wine with Errol Flynn, who rented The Barrymore guesthouse—the same room that became 1970s Butterfields restaurant—or hear Pendry's Wolfgang Puck whisper to the Butterfield's busboy Gerardo Olvera words of encouragement to take over the kitchen and open 1995 Olvera's.

Through such a portal, perhaps we would meet 1968s Arthur Blessit, shouldering his 12' cross while drinking coffee in conversation with the '90s local icon, WeHo Jesus (Kevin Lee Light).

In our time loop there's 2015s Steel Panthers closing the doors to House of Blues, stepping through to 2023s Bar Pendry to use the Moët & Chandon champagne vending machine.

Although no time portal actually exists, the otherworldly geometric artwork in the Pendry's lobby, *70' Icosahedron* by Anthony James, will blow your mind (and may convince you that time travel is possible)!

Pomegranate Fizz

The Boil:
Simple Syrup:
(Good for one month in the fridge, enough for twelve cocktails.)
Combine ¼ cup sugar with ¼ cup water and bring to a simmer;
stir until the sugar is completely dissolved and then remove pan from heat.

The Prep:
Juice and fine strain one lime (enough for one cocktail).
Juice and fine strain one pomegranate (enough for four cocktails).

The Mix:
1.5 oz Absolut Elyx Vodka
.5 oz dry curaçao
.25 oz simple syrup
.75 oz pomegranate juice
.75 oz lime juice
1 egg white*
1 oz Fever-Tree Soda Water

The Process:
Combine all ingredients, except soda, in a mixing tin and shake with ice.
Strain off the ice and dry shake; pour into a coupe glass and top with soda water.

The Fandangle:
Garnish with an expressed lemon peel.

The Creator:
Pendry West Hollywood's Team

FEVER-TREE

West
Hollywood

9015 Sunset Blvd.

The Nugget: *"It's called The Rainbow, The Bow, or The Rainbow Bar & Grill. Not the Rainbow Room*, that's in New York and doesn't have the same Rock 'n' Roll pedigree or music history to it."*

—Ace Von Johnson, LA Guns.

For the full history on the Rainbow Bar & Grill, stream the 2019 rockumentary *The Rainbow* directed by Zak Knutson on Amazon Prime Video.

The Tudor-style building at 9015 Sunset Boulevard was constructed in 1935 and home to an English-themed nightclub known as The Queen. The popular spot became Café Esquire in 1936, then Ray Haller's Mermaid Club in 1937. Villa Nova opened in 1940 and held the space until 1967. It re-opened as the Windjammer, which closed in 1971. The Rainbow opened the following year, and in 2022 celebrated its 50th anniversary!

*Note: "The Rainbow Room NY is INCREDIBLY historically important in the world of cocktails."—Sarah L.M. Mengoni

Jack & Coke

A.K.A. THE LEMMY
Honoring Lemmy Kilmister of the band Motörhead; this was his drink.

The Mix:
1.5 oz (or to taste) Jack Daniel's Tennessee Whiskey
Coca-Cola

The Process:
Add ice to a bucket glass, pour in the Jack Daniel's and then fill with Coke.

The Finish:
Give it a little stir so the Jack and the Coke become one.

THE
SUNSET
STRIP

I'd rather be dead than cool

8911 Sunset Blvd.

⟫⟫

The Nugget: The Moscow Mule was invented on The Sunset Strip, three tenths of a mile across the road at the dearly departed Cock'n Bull, 9170 Sunset Boulevard.

The invention kicked off in the 1940s with a friendship between John Martin, a vodka distributor, and Cock'n Bull owner, Jack Morgan. John had an oversupply of his vodka, (gin was the liquor of choice at the time) and Jack couldn't get rid of his homemade Ginger Beer for love or money. From that day on, the two failed beverages, combined in an engraved copper mug, have become infamously sipped around the world.

From the Cock'n Bull, The Moscow Mule made an "Irish Exit" (switching from vodka to whisky), where it dodged the traffic on Sunset Boulevard, and made it into the cocktail menu at Rock & Reilly's, along with the *Ex-Wife**!

8911 was formerly The Cat Club and the Galaxy Overflow (See Justin Queso's SS | 129 for more details).

*A cocktail which cost $250,000, and includes "everything behind the bar, payable in monthly installments for the rest of your life."

Irish Mule

The Prep:
Juice and fine strain one lime (enough for one cocktail).

The Mix:
2 oz Tullamore D.E.W. Original Irish Whiskey
.5 oz lime juice
6 oz Fever-Tree Ginger Beer

The Process:
Combine all ingredients in a copper mug filled with ice, stir.

The Fandangle:
Garnish with a lime wheel.

The Creator:
This modern classic was chosen for the bar's cocktail menu by Reilly o'Reilly.

FEVER-TREE

THE
**SUNSET
STRIP**

Tonights The Night...

9009 Sunset Blvd.

The Nugget: Fifty years ago, Lou Adler, had an opportunity to create a space for rock concerts. That bet paid off. The Roxy Theatre needs no introductions. It is a legendary venue, which celebrated its anniversary in September 2023.

As a transplant, you come to LA to pursue one thing and often opportunities arise for another—if you are open to it. The Roxy is a place of opportunity, as Tina Karras, founder of Tina's Vodka discovered.

In 1997, with two suitcases and a guitar slung over her shoulder, Tina moved to LA from Charlotte, NC. One night at The Roxy, after her performance, Tina had a chance encounter that led to a part-time job at the venue. Her evolving position led Tina to strong relationships with liquor reps and distributors. She soon found a gap in the market, specifically for female-owned organic vodka (that was also non-GMO, super clean, and delicious). Welcome to Tina's Vodka. Tina's first love will always be music but there is no denying that the universe showed her that she could do more!

9009 Sunset Boulevard was built in 1935 by architect Harold Johnson and was home to Westside Market for 18 years. From 1950-1972 the building transformed into a "class" burlesque house called Largo.

Tina's Delight

The Boil:
Simple Syrup:
(Good for one month in the fridge, enough for 24 cocktails.)
Combine ½ cup sugar with ½ cup water in a pan and bring to a simmer;
stir until the sugar is completely dissolved and then remove from heat.

The Prep:
Juice and fine strain one lime (enough for two cocktails).

The Mix:
1.5 oz Tina's Vodka
.25 oz simple syrup
1 oz pineapple juice
.5 oz lime
1 oz ginger ale

The Process:
Combine all ingredients, except ginger ale, in a mixing tin and shake with ice.
Strain into a highball glass and top with ginger ale
(for a really authentic rock club experience put it in a plastic party cup).

The Fandangle:
Throw a lime wedge in it.

The Creator:
Nathan Jenisch

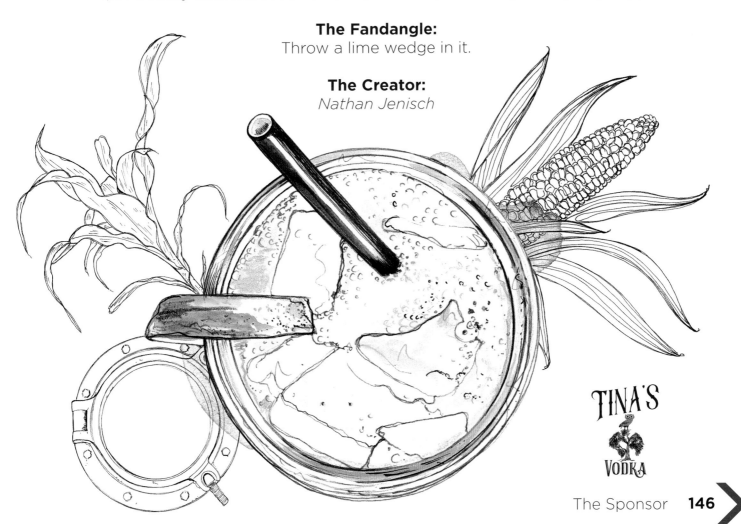

TINA'S
VODKA

SKYBAR
LOS ANGELES

MONDRIAN
LOS ANGELES

8440 Sunset Blvd.

The Nugget: *"It's no use going back to yesterday, because I was a different person then."*
—Lewis Carroll, Alice's Adventures in Wonderland.

8840 Sunset Boulevard had many yesterdays, from a 1930 mansion-converted-school to the 12-floor, 1961 Braemar Towers apartments building. In 1984, LA Times announced a "New Hotel to Serve as Artist Giant Canvas" with the L'Hommage Mondrian painted by Israeli artist Jaacov Agam.

In 1996 it started the journey to today's wonderland-inspired Mondrian, white washing the wall back to a gallery standard. Curious and curiouser are the mood-lit hotel hallways with light boxes featuring Los Angeles-born light artist, James Turrell. Giant doors face The Sunset Strip providing a playful entrance into a world of distorted scale. In 2022, the Mondrian LA partnered with Artlounge Collective for curated bi-monthly exhibitions in the lobby's Magic Box featuring local artists and mural concepts.

The Skybar, a flirty companion to the Mondrian LA was, in yesteryears, described as "where the beautiful people schmooze and booze." Still true today, the poolside paradise has stood the White Rabbit test of time.

The Red Headed Mule

The Boil:
Simple Syrup:
(Good for one month in the fridge, enough for ten cocktails.)
Combine ½ cup sugar with ½ cup water and bring to a simmer;
stir until the sugar is completely dissolved and then remove the pan from heat.

The Prep:
Juice and fine strain one lemon (enough for two cocktails).

The Mix:
2 oz Kettle One Vodka
.5 oz simple syrup
.5 oz fresh lemon juice
6 muddled raspberries
Q Mixers Ginger Beer

The Process:
Muddle raspberries in a mixing tin; add the other ingredients and shake with ice.
Strain into a copper mug filled with fresh ice and top with ginger beer.

The Fandangle:
Garnish with two skewered raspberries.

The Creator:
Aidan Marus

Q
MIXERS

West
Hollywood

Ketel One®
VODKA

State

SOCIAL HOUSE

8782 Sunset Blvd.

The Nugget: Many things can be written about the property where the State Social House resides—especially as the building, in 1952, housed the Screen Writers Guild.

Woody Harrelson's Oxygen (O2) with a vegan raw bar menu once sat in this space. Ironically this former O2 inhaling bar was flipped into The Backroom, a smoking lounge. Owner Robert Silverberg defied convention and challenged the City of West Hollywood to operate a fully licensed smoking venue. The space is known today as the Tortugo Tasting & Smoking Lounge, a treasure on The Strip.

The structure is a combination of three original spaces. Two were completed in 1935 and the third in 1938. Collectively, the building has been home to many, such as Old World Inn, Grappa, Da Pasquale, Red Rock, and Tangerine.

Cigar Pairing

The Mix:
1 Ashton Cabinet Selection Cigar
1 glass of Tortugo Isabela White Ale
1 neat pour of The Macallan 12 yo Single Malt Scotch Whisky

The Process:
Cut the tip from your cigar and light it.

The Fandangle:
Grab an ashtray.

SUNSET MARQUIS

1200 Alta Loma Rd.

The Nugget: George Rosenthal, the founding owner of the Sunset Marquis Hotel & Villas, stated in 2014, "I don't paint, and I don't write music. A piece of property is the canvas on which I can create things." George achieved that when he closely modeled the Sunset Marquis on the ethos and free spirit of the Garden of Allah, demolished in 1959. Garden of Allah, sat on the fringe of WeHo, was silent film star Alla Nazimova's mansion-turned-hotel, and home to a veritable melting pot of creatives.

You can easily become discombobulated within minutes of stepping off the busy WeHo street and into the enchanted series of labyrinth pathways that connect Sunset Marquis. The hotel has a legacy beyond any words. If you want to nose-dive into rock history, like the Red Hot Chili Peppers did in 1992 from the roof of the hotel's third floor and into the pool, check out the book published in 2013 *If These Walls Could Rock: 50 Years at the Legendary Sunset Marquis Hotel!*

In 2023, the Sunset Marquis celebrated its 60th anniversary. It is also home to the NightBird Recording Studio, Cavatina Restaurant, Bar 1200, and the Morrison Hotel Gallery.

Honeydew Me

The Prep:
Tarragon Honeydew Mint Syrup:
(Good for one week in the fridge, enough for thirteen cocktails.)
Blend 1 cup honeydew melon, 1 tbsp of loosely packed fresh mint leaves,
3 tbsp of loosely packed fresh tarragon, ¾ cup sugar, and 5 oz water. Fine strain.

Juice and fine strain one lemon (enough for two cocktails).

The Mix:
2 oz Quechōl Sotol
.75 oz tarragon honeydew mint syrup
.5 oz lemon juice

The Process:
Combine all ingredients in a mixing tin and shake with ice;
strain into a rocks glass over fresh ice.

The Fandangle:
Garnish with a slice of watermelon radish.

The Creator:
Diego Marrero

West Hollywood

SOTOL QUECHŌL

TESSE

8500 Sunset Blvd.

The Nugget: The tagline from vodka brand Kástra Elión, is "A myth is in the unmaking." Their name in English roughly translates to castle and olives. To unmake their vodka, you'll find it is sourced from Greek olives grown in a grove that overlooks a castle from the owner's ancestral home.

Name play is also a staple for the cocktails at Tesse. The original menu featured a Melon DeGeneres and today, under the creation of Heidi Wittekind and Kristina Cox, you can seasonally sip on the Pea Diddy or Bad Bunny!

Tesse is a derivative from the French word *délicatesse*. Before this dynamic and inclusive space was constructed from the ground up, the marquee of the 1958 built former building read Dino's Lodge. Dino's took the nickname, likeness, and caricature of Dean Martin and was featured in the opening sequence of the TV series, *77 Sunset Strip*.

In 1966, east of Dino's, we would have seen the Seawitch and to the west, the Tiffany Theatre. In 1977, the movie theater became the original place where you could dress up and watch *The Rocky Horror Picture Show*. The Tiffany sign can be found today at the Valley Relics Museum located in the San Fernando Valley.

Pea Diddy

The Wait:
Pea Husk Juice:
Remove peas from 8 oz of English peas, then soak the empty shells
(can substitute snap or snow pea pods) in water for 24 hours, then juice
(In a blender 8 oz of pea shells yields 3 oz of juice, a juicer will yield more).

The Prep:
Mint Syrup:
(Good for one month in the fridge, enough for eight cocktails.)
Put 4, loosely packed, tbsp mint in boiling water for 45 seconds;
pull mint from hot water and place in an ice bath.
Once it's cold, blend the blanched mint with ¾ cup simple syrup, fine strain,
and then strain again through cheesecloth.

Juice and fine strain one lime (enough for one cocktail).

The Mix:
1.5 oz Kástra Elión Vodka
.25 oz Svöl Swedish-Style Aquavit
.25 oz Meletti Anisette
2 oz pea husk juice
.75 oz mint syrup
.5 oz lime juice
1 oz soda water

The Process:
Combine all ingredients in a mixing tin and shake with ice.
Add 1 oz soda water then strain into a footed highball glass filled with fresh ice.

The Fandangle:
Garnish with all things pea. Tendrils, butterflied snap peas, pea flowers.

The Creator:
Heidi Wittekind and Kristina Cox

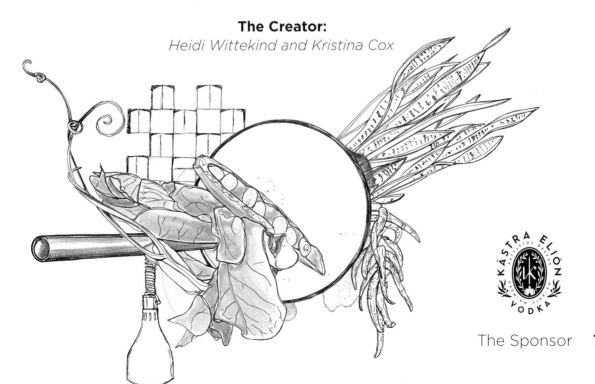

Sunset Tower Hotel

8358 Sunset Blvd.

➤➤➤

The Nugget: Leland A. Bryant was the architect for three buildings in West Hollywood. The most acclaimed, Sunset Tower, was added to the National Register of Historical Places in 1980. The Tower is considered as one of the finest examples of Zigzag Moderne Art Deco architecture in the world.

The Sunset Tower opened in 1929 as a 46-unit luxury apartment house. It was one of the first California structures to be earthquake proof and "all-electric". In 1970, the owners began a long eviction process to "smash" the joint down. One tenant, *Hogan's Heroes* actor, Werner Klemperer, refused to leave. This defiance saved the Tower from demolition. The cocktail's name honors that bulldozing threat!

In 1986 the property was converted into a hotel and briefly renamed Argyle Hotel. The original name was reinstalled with hotelier Jeff Klein in 2005, whose vision brought us the Tower Bar, which was the former pied-à-terre of gangster Ben "Bugsy" Seigel.

Tower Smash

The Boil:
Simple Syrup:
(Good for one month in fridge, enough for six cocktails.)
Combine ½ cup sugar with ½ cup water and bring to a simmer;
stir until the sugar is completely dissolved, then remove pan from heat.

The Prep:
Juice and fine strain one lemon (enough for one cocktail).

The Mix:
2 oz reposado tequila
.75 oz simple syrup
1 oz lemon juice
3-5 basil leaves
ginger beer

The Process:
Gently muddle the basil in a mixing tin then combine all ingredients except ginger beer
and shake with ice. Fine strain into a rocks glass and top with ginger beer.

The Fandangle:
Garnish with a lemon wheel resting on a beautiful basil leaf.

The Creator:
Brett Zimmerman

West Hollywood

WARRIOR

8909 Sunset Blvd.

➤➤➤

The Nugget: Warrior Bar opened in 2019 with a magical patio oasis that celebrated a spectacular view of the city. Unfortunately, the bar is now closed but luckily for us, it's transformed into an event space for hire. *Once Upon a Cocktail* book launch parties, anyone?

The original construction at 8909 Sunset Boulevard was completed in 1937. The second floor, which hosts that classic view, was added in 2013. Thank you, Pearl's Rooftop, for your service to swanky renovations.

This particular block on The Strip can often be historically confusing—good luck untangling the dynamic history of what was where. Research suggests there have been many lives to 8909; it was, once upon a time, Dukes Coffee Shop (see kitchen24 RD | 71 for more details), Sneeky Pete's, The Unicorn Coffee House, Splash Deli, and a school for dramatic arts. These and more have called this infamous address home.

Morning Glory

The Wait:
(Good for two weeks in the fridge, enough for four cocktails.)
Put 4 tbsp of Frosted Flakes cereal into 8 oz of Toki Japanese Whisky,
cover and let sit overnight. Fine strain.

The Boil:
Simple Syrup:
(Good for one month in the fridge, enough for lots of cocktails.)
Combine ¼ cup sugar with ¼ cup water and bring to a simmer;
stir until the sugar is completely dissolved and then remove the pan from heat.

The Mix:
2 oz Frosted Flakes-infused Suntory Toki Japanese Whisky
1 bar spoon simple syrup
3 dashes orange bitters

The Process:
Combine all ingredients in a mixing glass and stir with ice,
then strain into a rocks glass over a big ice cube.

The Fandangle:
Garnish with a burnt orange peel.

The Creator:
David Gonzales

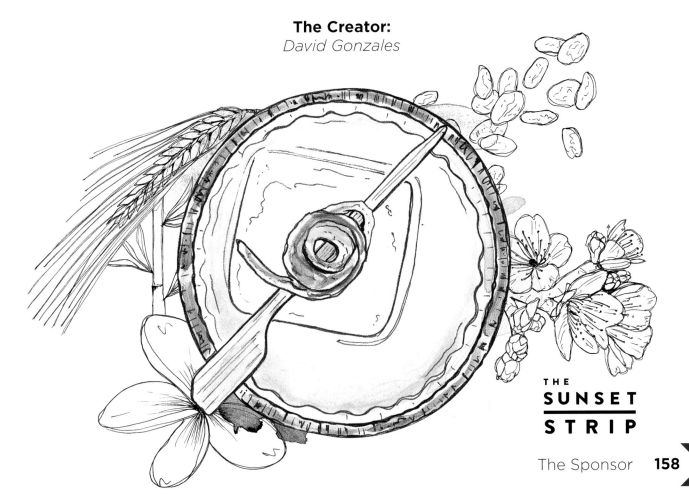

THE SUNSET STRIP

Life Hack (LH) | Featuring Katie Brightside

Katie Brightside

What qualifies me to write this section you say? Nothing actually. But who puts a Life Hack section in a cocktail book? Someone who understands the importance of balance, yet at the same time finds that tricky to obtain. Isn't that called being human?

If we had an answer to feeling good, wouldn't we all be taking the cure? For years I have been on a personal quest to understand happiness and feeling good. For me it doesn't exist as a pot of gold at the end of a rainbow. However, it can be caught moment to moment as long as, collectively, the glimmers are mostly joy. That my friends, is the fountain of youth. Tomorrow is a new beginning; I can't control the future, just the now.

Happiness comes easier to me when my body and mind are in alignment. As I get older, I practice being kind to myself. I like to take care of the vessel that houses my organs. This can be as easy as drinking more water and sleeping a full night—the simple Life Hacks.

I was eight when I did my first walkathon, a marathon-distance trek around my hometown. As an only child, I did what my parents did. As this was the '80s, we didn't stretch after, replace electrolytes, or even drink water. After the event, I remember the hurt in my body felt like the worst flu. Since then, I have run actual marathons, a super marathon, jumped out of a plane, lived in four countries, attended a silent retreat, completed a 90-day hot yoga challenge, used floatation tanks, hypnotherapy, acupuncture, LED therapy, sweat therapy, cryotherapy, and so much more... In all that time, the best advice I've received was from my Australian Osteopathy practitioner, Gary Choi, which was reinforced by my American Chiropractor, Michael Tebbe, DC. They both suggested a maintenance plan to keep on top of body annoyances or ailments before they manifest into a bigger issue. That lesson was hard to learn during my marathon years. Once in Australia, I was sitting on the loo (toilet) stretching my upper body and I pulled muscle in my neck. It took weeks of treatment to recover. From that day on I have always listened to how I'm feeling and acted accordingly. I do invest time to feel the best I can.

The moral of the story is, be the best friend you can be to yourself. Have you heard of the oxygen mask theory? Put your own on first, then you can best assist others.

On the following pages I will introduce a few tricks I used on this book, whether it was during R+D for the book (aka cocktail tasting) or helping with stress levels while under a deadline to compile the book. These are a few West Hollywood businesses that promote health and wellbeing and a few of my personal Life Hacks.

8365 Santa Monica Blvd.

earthbar®

The Nugget: The original wooden sign from Great Earth Vitamins graces the front of 8365 Santa Monica Boulevard's Earthbar store, a nod to its humble beginnings; Great Earth Vitamins first opened in Tarzana in 1971. Not long after, a second store followed in Larchmont. After a brand overhaul in 2007, the flagship Earthbar, as we know it today, supplies all sorts of life hacks to aid a sense of equilibrium.

The strip mall, where WeHo Earthbar is located, was constructed in 1966. The former property was an influential 200 round, seated live theater in 1950 called *The Players Ring*. Six years later, it was home to a production of *Tea and Sympathy*, starring Michael Landan alongside an up-and-coming 19-year-old Jack Nicholson. The theater closed its doors in 1964 after a suspected arson attack, which left only the front wall of the structure and the marquee unscathed. Producer Paul Levitt continued to operate plays down the road at the newly christened *The Players' Ring* at 8325 Santa Monica Boulevard. Today, this venue is known as the Coast Playhouse. After many years of dormant theatrics, the City of West Hollywood is set to revive the theater in our near future.

Liver Cleanse

The Prep:
If you know you're going to have a late night of drinking, make this recipe before the fun starts
(then you'll only have to fight through your fuzzy head enough to get to the fridge).
When you do make it ahead of time,
double strain the pith out to keep the drink from going brown.

The Mix:
Approx. 2 medium or 1 ½ large green apples (9 oz juice)
Approx. 1 whole beet (6 oz juice)
Approx. 1 whole lemon (1 oz juice)
Approx. 3 ½" piece ginger (.5 oz juice)
1 oz aloe vera juice

The Process:
Juice all the ingredients above together.

The Finish:
Pour the liver cleanse into your most comforting drinking vessel
and get out there and reclaim your day!
Or, go back to bed and binge watch your favorite show.

The Creators:
Noah Bubman & Maryam Hooshim

City of West Hollywood
California 1984

Infrared Sauna

Next Health has devised a *One Stop Shop* to help you look and feel your best before hitting the town and to prevent any lingering effects of your late-night adventures the next day.

The Nugget: *One-Stop-Shop*, Part 1, Infrared Sauna Pod. The Next Health Sauna Capsule is a whole-body treatment to do the day of your event or big night out. The heat is evenly distributed through the body with both near and far-infrared light frequencies. This generates a sweat that can increase metabolic function, relaxation, and support deep detoxification. The light also enhances collagen production, cellular regeneration, and combats inflammation. These benefits are a perfect combination to help you look and feel your best.

Light has been a source of healing since the dawn of time. The Ancient Egyptians built temples and covered the exposed openings with special cloths to distort the light. In 1800, Sir William Herschel experimented with a prism to disperse the sun's light into different colors. He measured the heat of each color, which grew hotter from blue to red and by chance, he placed the thermometer just above the red into a region not seen with the naked eye, now known as infrared. In 1818 France, hospitals were designed with open spaces to let in more sun rays to aid with mental health. In 1903 a Nobel Prize winning scientist, Niel Finsen, adapted ultraviolet 'electric' light, which avoided sunlight burning the skin while retaining its antibacterial effects. As research progressed, lasers were developed to harness the light to a single beam to heal site-specific areas. Rapid advancements in technology in recent years brought us LED's (Light Emitting Diodes), a semiconductor device that emits light when a current flows through it. Each wavelength produces a different colored light—or in the case of infrared, invisible, like the Sir William Herschel experiment. The varying light and frequencies penetrate the skin tissue at different depths, energizing the cells, and healing different ailments.

While in West Hollywood, book an Infrared Sauna at Next Health. If you are away from The Creative City, consider a direct infrared therapy such as the Celluvation PCN pen for spot treatments.

IGNITE YOUR FIRE

NEXT|HEALTH®

8570 Sunset Blvd. Suite 6.1A

Hangover IV Drip

The Nugget: *One-Stop-Shop*, Part 2, Hangover IV Therapy. The biggest revelation from the Next Health team was that I had been doing it wrong all these years. I was nurturing the aftereffects of a good night out rather than preventing the extreme of the aftermath symptoms. Bingo! Not only does having a drip the day of a big night out make you more sparkly but you don't have to crawl to the nearest drip bar when you feel worse-for-wear the next day.

Why did I put an IV drip in the book? The intravenous bag includes a multivitamin base*, also known as the Myers' Cocktail (there is it, the word cocktail!). This cocktail has lysine and taurine, which encourage the elimination of toxins and harmful substances in the body while supporting the detoxification pathways. Moreover, the drip has a powerful concoction of hydrating electrolytes, vitamins, amino acids, and more; it's also administered by a registered nurse!

Studies show the vitamins and amino acids included in the Hangover IV may increase levels of antioxidants (glutathione) in the body that not only help eliminate toxins, but accelerate the recovery and repair processes that need extra support when you're hungover. The Hangover IV replenishes nutrients and fluid that will or have been lost during a long night out. Remember, an ounce of prevention is better than a pound of a cure! Whether you do a drip before or after a bender, any help is good help.

*Multivitamin base contains B12, Chromium, B-complex, Vitamin C, Zinc, Copper, Calcium, and Magnesium.

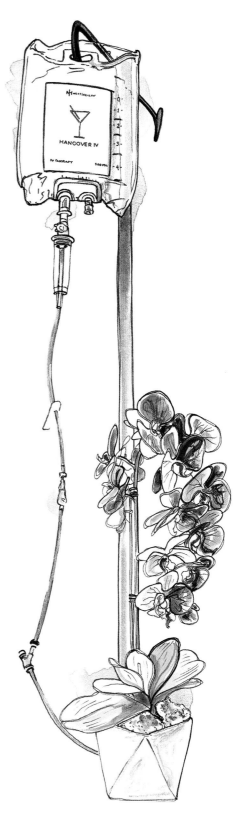

NEXT | HEALTH®

8570 Sunset Blvd. Suite 6.1A

THE
SUNSET
STRIP

Cryotherapy

The Nugget: *One-Stop-Shop*, Part 3, Cryotherapy has had a long and arduous history to have progressed to a state-of-the-art Next Health chamber.

The Egyptians used cold to treat injuries and inflammation. Through grueling experimentation, cold therapy was used to treat a wide variety of ailments. Today's non-nitrogen, whole-body Cryotherapy is not scary in the slightest—it's just bloody cold. The-150 degrees Fahrenheit chill makes your blood vessels constrict, moving blood away from the limbs, toward the vital organs, which in return triggers healing and boosts the immune system. It could be said that it activates, without harm, the fight or flight response in a three minute thirty second session where the body gets sent into overdrive to repair itself and jump starts the release of norepinephrine (the goddess of feel-good endorphins) into the bloodstream.

Why does this work as part three of the *One-Stop-Shop*? It will super boost the other two treatments and elevate your mood before hitting your night out on the town. It may also aid in athletic recovery time, decrease inflammation, boost collagen, and enhance immunity.

Essentially, if I do this trio before painting-the-town-red, it helps take the steam out of my dusty head the next day!

*Please seek advice from a professional health provider before treatments.

NH NEXT|HEALTH®
8570 Sunset Blvd. Suite 6.1A

Ophora Water

The Nugget: #DrinkMeWeHo

Water is the elixir of life and hydration is a key to surviving a dusty head. Drinking H_2O regularly—while painting the town red—will aid and elevate against future dehydration. Keeping your water levels balanced leads to feeling less of a prune the next day.

To charge the body back to a more superhuman condition, my Life Hack 101 is Ophora Water which is hyper-oxygenated (four times more than regular water). This premium, bottled water will fast-track cellular hydration, increase energy, and enhance immune function. With four US patents the technology removes damaging chemicals to bring you the water as nature intended—pure. Ophora is a mashup of O-oxygen PH-pH balanced ORA-gold standard. So Ophora literally means liquid gold. Pick up this award-winning water at your nearest Erewhon or direct from orphorawater.com.

OPHORA

WATER FOR WELLNESS®

NANO · PURE®
RE-STRUCTURED®
HYPER-OXYGENATED®

750 mL (25.4 FL OZ)

OPHORA

ophorawater.com

Build Your Own (BYO) | Featuring Jackie Subeck

In the mid-2010s I experienced one of those moments that so many others, of *a certain age*, have encountered–it was time to reinvent myself again. After spending the better part of three decades in the Los Angeles music industry and breaking down formerly walled off entertainment doors and opportunities in what was then, a newly emerging China, I knew it was time for a major change. After much research (yes, I Googled "Lists of Careers") and hours of deep introspection (I work fast), I came to realize that my longtime companion and frequent best friend cannabis, was budding (the puns are never-ending) into an actual commercial industry. It was 2014 and after twenty years of a quasi-regulated medical cannabis underground marketplace, legalization in California was starting to take shape. I decided to jump on board. But where would I fit? I wasn't a doctor, or a scientist, a product maker, or a farmer. How would my prior life experience connect with the quickly evolving industry that was forming around this remarkable plant I had been enjoying for decades?

Written by Jackie Subeck | Cannabis Policy Advocate & Consumption Lounge Owner

Jackie Subeck

Although I didn't figure it out for another two years, I was certain of one undeniable fact. Music and weed (can I call it that now?) go together. Like rock and roll. Like campfires and s'mores. Like Bert and Ernie. The dots were connected, but they were buried deep under more than fifty years of reefer madness, stigma, and antiquated assumptions about the dangers of cannabis. I knew I had to get in there and break down some doors, so I took a leadership role in Los Angeles with a group called Women Grow and began hosting business networking events at West Hollywood spots including J. Gerard, owned by the remarkable Lady J, and The Abbey, one of WeHo's crown jewels, both of whom were *willing* to become partners. These venues allowed us to bring cannabis knowledge, education, and innovative product samples to their establishments well before legalization gave us the freedom to do so. I quickly joined the Prop 64 campaign, which would eventually legalize cannabis in California, and next thing I knew, it was November 2016 and it had passed!

From medical marijuana in 1996 to adult-use cannabis in 2016, West Hollywood has been front and center on cannabis and having lived here for more than two and a half decades, I knew it was the spot to build up an exciting marketplace. Having solved my existential crisis of who I was going to be in this industry, I met with some of my councilmembers and pitched the idea of legal cannabis consumption lounges–social establishments where adults could legally consume cannabis without fear of judgment, stigma or worse, arrest, and hopefully with music, comedy and other forms of entertainment alongside. With hundreds of existing bars and restaurants, this didn't seem like a far-fetched idea, but it came with many unpredictable twists. After dozens of meetings, discussions, and brainstorming sessions, the West Hollywood City Council passed the cannabis ordinance, including consumption lounges, in November 2017, bringing those connected underground dots to the surface.

I believe cannabis lounges are the future. After more than forty years of a War on Drugs that branded cannabis as a dangerous substance, adults can finally socialize and enjoy nightlife with cannabis rather than alcohol. We knew going in that there was no lack of potential customers, but also that we had to create special experiences to attract them in and make them feel safe–something that's been impossible to do until now. Folks coming to West Hollywood are now able to find nearly a dozen beautiful dispensaries to shop in along with exciting consumption lounges, some with full-service restaurants, music, and entertainment, to consume in as places to enjoy a yummy pre-roll, a hard-hitting dab, or a low-dose cannabis-infused mocktail. Early on we even talked about a shuttle that would take guests around to visit several different lounges without having to get behind the wheel. Now that's a shuttle I can stand behind!

If I were to offer one insight to anyone wishing to visit a cannabis consumption lounge, it would be this. When considering government and science, it is helpful to remind yourself that what we cannot do today, we will surely be able to do tomorrow. Given the natural inclination towards inclusivity and community in WeHo, it is my hope that all of the businesses in our city, no matter what type they are, will get on board and support our growing network of small cannabis businesses.

The cannabis industry is complicated and challenging–not gonna lie–and given the incessant roadblocks, what these groups have done to bring our lounges to life is bordering on remarkable. Cannabis brings people together–it always has. Come to WeHo and have a puff or two with us!

The Nugget: Since the word cocktail is associated with alcohol being present in a beverage, these non-alcoholic cannabis-infused drinks are often called mocktails. As the word generally suggests that a drink is intoxicant free, we feel mocktail is inaccurate and have chosen not to use it.

The ever-evolving California cannabis laws currently forbid THC drinks like our Build Your Own from being made in a cannabis consumption lounge. Fortunately you can order from a wide selection of regulated "sealed" cans of CBD and THC infused beverages.

With the BYO cocktail, Sarah and I wanted to create a ritualized way of consuming a THC drink that has the old-skool feel of sitting around a table with friends rolling joints or packing bowls. Not that either of us have ever experienced such a ritual (nudge nudge wink wink)!

Check out the Tasting Note on page 178 for the scoop on the creation of the Build Your Own THC Experience.

Build Your Own

The Prep:
Juice and fine strain 1/8 of a large watermelon (enough for two drinks).

The Mix:
1 drop* ALT THC tincture
(Pick One)
1 small sprig of cilantro
3 or 4 mint leaves
1 thin slice of jalapeño
(Pick One)
3 oz pomegranate juice (POM)
3 oz watermelon juice
3 oz soda water

The Process:
This one is up to you!
All of these ingredients work well together, so try experimenting with different combinations.
First, choose between the jalapeño or one of the fresh herbs, then pick a juice.
Put both in a rocks glass filled with ice, then add the soda water
and the tincture and gently stir the drink to mix it all together.

The Exploration:
This is fun to do with friends! Play around with the different ingredients, see who likes what.
You can even explore other options!
Many different ingredients may taste great with your tincture.
Try other juices, sodas, fresh ingredients,
or anything in your garden or kitchen (but the sink) that inspires you.
Choosing your own THC drinking adventure knows no boundaries but those you set!

The Creator:
Sarah L.M. Mengoni

* Different tinctures have different potencies, so use at your own discretion and/or consult
with a knowledgeable budtender at your local cannabis shop.

During our marathon research and developement (R+D) sessions, I did more than just taste cocktails… I took notes! The point was to capture something about the experience in words to help you understand the drinks, spaces, and people better. These are those notes.

DESIGN DISTRICT

DD | 29

Catch LA | *Detox Retox*
You arrive at Catch through an open-air entry dripping with greenery and flowers (you actually have to push them aside!). When the retractable ceiling is pulled back you dine under the clear LA sky. That's quite an experience for a cocktail to measure up to but Detox Retox does. Fresh cucumber is what's dominant and matcha brings great flavor, while providing texture (an often-overlooked aspect of cocktails), and a nice earthiness that matches well with the Código 1530 Blanco Tequila.

DD | 31

Cecconi's West Hollywood | *Lychee Martini*
Julia the cocktail's creator, who goes by Jools in her singing career, was inspired by her love of Lychee Martinis to develop one for her guests. She did the hard work of researching these specialty Martinis at several bars before coming up with her own pitch-perfect version. Like Julia, the lychee in this drink sings. Cecconi's Lychee Martini is silky, powerful, and delicious!

DD | 33

Craig's | *Danny Ocean*
Craig's feels like new old Hollywood with their classic-style leather booths, low lights, and dark wood. The gray brick and contemporary photos provide a new twist on a time-honored theme. This cocktail fits in perfectly. It's made using the George Clooney co-founded Casamigos Reposado Tequila, which provides depth of flavor to this cocktail, whose recipe uses classic proportions. The jalapeño and basil additions hint toward modern cocktail culture.

DD | 35

E.P. + L.P. | *Where Love Lives*
If you live in Los Angeles, you probably know the delights of fruitas, fresh tropical fruit cut before your eyes at impossibly small umbrella covered carts. The fruit is scooped into a container and covered in lime and Tajin, a spicy, citrusy, salty, granulated substance that is divine. THIS COCKTAIL TASTES LIKE FRUITAS, with the addition of El Silencio Mezcal. I love it and since it's their bestselling cocktail, by a wide margin, it seems the drinking public also agrees.

DD | 37

Gracias Madre | *Aguachile*
The relaxed, rustic vibe you get at this upscale vegan restaurant would never lead you to think that most of the drinks here are created using very modern cocktail technology. In fact, the Aguachile is basically the only one you can make at home without buying all kinds of expensive (and sizable) new toys. Yet it still takes some fancy techniques to get its wonderful texture and unusual combination of flavors, so this is the perfect cocktail to impress your friends! The tart, lightly spicy, slightly sweet flavors of the Cascahuín Tequila 48, Kalani Coconut Liqueur, and the other ingredients evolve in your mouth as you drink it. This one is not to be missed.

DD | 39

Issima (R.I.P.) | *Barcelona*
Issima takes its inspiration from Mediterranean food and drinks to deliver cuisine and cocktails that reflect both Europe and West Hollywood. The Barcelona is a Spanish Gin-Tonic fancified by creator Melina Meza. Light, refreshing, and distinctly floral, this is a gin cocktail that will win over vodka drinkers. Don't use a straw, put your nose in the glass and smell the flowers!

DD | 41

La Peer Hotel | *Whiskey Colada*
We all know that rum goes great with coconut and pineapple—well so does whiskey! Many whiskeys have tropical notes that make them a delicious match for tropical cocktails. Using both Glen Grant Scotch and Wild Turkey 101 Rye adds layers of complexity to this drink, the Kalani Coconut Liqueur adds a fantastic flavor that comes from actual coconuts and bitters balance its sweetness.

DD | 43   *Misdirecting Travelers*
This juicy, bittersweet cocktail was inspired by the 1970s tropical classic, the Jungle Bird. It deliciously switches out the rum in the original for Monkey 47 Gin and a touch of allspice dram. The name, incidentally, is a nod to the great horror film, *The Birds*, where the protagonist describes her work at an airport as... misdirecting travelers.

DD | 45   *Vegan Daiquiri Jello Shots*
This take on an old, house-party fave creates a truly sophisticated shot. Modeled after the classic Daiquiri cocktail, Appleton Estate Signature Rum and the addition of Kalani Coconut Liqueur make these shots tasty and fun. Because Agar Agar is used in place of gelatin, no animals are harmed in the making.

DD | 47   *Working Title*
The whiskey in this cocktail is the brainchild of LA native Andrew Borenzweig. Every sip is complex, boozy, and delicious. The Beverly High Rye Whiskey shines through. It has distinct peach notes that blend really nicely with the drink's other main ingredients, aged peach brandy and maraschino liqueur.

DD | 49   *Savage Journey*
This cocktail is so many things—smoky from the Del Maguey Vida Mezcal, sweet from the St-Germain Elderflower Liqueur, bitter from the Salers Gentiane Aperitif, and boozy from all the above. It's a journey of flavor that may not take you where you were planning but it will certainly take you somewhere. As it has been said, "Buy the ticket, take the ride."

DD | 51   *Turn Up*
Whether you have this Espresso Martini with the traditional Grey Goose Vodka or with trendy 818 Añejo Tequila, it will help keep your party vibe going. Caffè Borghetti Espresso Liqueur is very rich and silky, and has a generous amount of caffeine, so between it and the espresso you really will be turnt!

DD | 53   **Le Parc at Melrose |** *1542*
Whether you're enjoying this light and crisp cocktail at the pool or in the bar, it will surely refresh you. Cucumber dominates and works great with the spicy peppers and tajin. The Old Harbor Gin they're using is made in San Diego with botanicals sourced from Southern California. This drink is so good that you may want to move in. Luckily you can, since this hotel also has residences.

DD | 55   **Olivetta |** *Dirty Blue Martini*
Are you the type of person who can't get enough blue cheese stuffed olives in your Martini? Then here's the drink for you! This cocktail takes the blue cheese out of the olive and puts it into the booze. It's a bold take on a modern classic.
Kat the bartender (who had great bangs when we visited her) says, "The Espresso Martini is the best!" and with their addition of cocoa, it really is quite yummy.

DD | 57   **Soulmate |** *Soulmate*
Naomi Schimek, Soulmate Bar Director and longtime influencer of Los Angeles beverage culture, uses plants native to California and supports spirits owned by women, LGBTQ+ entrepreneurs, and other members of traditionally marginalized communities in her cocktail menus. Elegant and complex, but still simple and easy to sip, this really well-made drink uses a California species of bay leaf and Amass, a gin made in Downtown LA by distiller Morgan McLachlan.
Having Fanny Flutters is never a bad thing; drop by Soulmate to see what we mean.

DD | 59   **SUR |** *The Rainbow*
This cocktail is light, fresh, and simple. The combo of Veev Açaí Spirit, basil, and house made strawberry purée drinks like a summer breeze. The restaurant itself is dazzlingly beautiful, unique, and eclectic; it may also have the comfiest bar stools in all of West Hollywood. Fans from around the world know SUR as the home of Vanderpump Rules. Stassie, on the show, made their fried goat cheese balls (SO good) famous; SUR donates a portion of the money made from their sale to a different charity every month.

Written by Sarah L.M. Mengoni

RAINBOW DISTRICT

RD | 65

The Abbey Bar & Food | *Cooley Cosmo*
Dance, drink, and drool over exposed muscles! That's why you come to The Abbey. Just one of these boozy Cosmopolitans will get your visit to this iconic gay bar off to a fierce start.

RD | 67

Beaches WeHo | *Mango Tango Frozen Margarita*
If we're to accurately represent drinking in West Hollywood, we HAD to include a frozen cocktail! It seems like every spot in WeHo, from the diviest-dive to the craftiest cocktail bar, has a frozen machine. Beaches WeHo is producing a very tasty Frozen Mango Margarita. They use a mango purée that is actually made with real mangos and blanco tequila. The results are very authentic flavors that reflect this location's fun and flirty vibe.

RD | 69

Chamberlain West Hollywood | *Perrier-Jouët*
Lounging at a rooftop pool and sipping champagne is SO West Hollywood. This one offers a view of the Hollywood Hills and a lovely choice of champagne: tart, creamy, yeasty, and fruity Perrier-Jouët. A terrific way to spend an afternoon. Or an evening. Or a morning...

RD | 71

kitchen24 (Ramada by Wyndham) | *Irish Coffee*
One doesn't walk into this fabulous pink-hued diner expecting a decent bar, let alone a better-than-average drink, so kitchen24's Irish Coffee variation, and their well-stocked back bar, were wonderful surprises! Tullamore D.E.W. Irish Whiskey is a time-tested choice for this drink and California's St. George NOLA Coffee Liqueur is a great addition. Surprisingly, Los Angeles nights can be chilly but this drink will knock that chill right out of you. Even in warmer weather this drink is an excellent night-cap.

RD | 73

Montrose at Beverly Hills | *Untitled*
This silky, scrumptious cocktail is packed with more than just booze and aromatics, it's also overflowing with multicultural history. Dewar's White Label Blended Scotch Whisky is the main ingredient in the cocktail. The Dewar's brand started as a grocer's shop way back in 1846. There, John Dewar started creating his own whisky blends. The amaro in this cocktail brings bitter-sweet flavors. A distinctly Italian spirit, amaro goes back to the Middle Ages when Italians were just getting into the swing of distillation; bitters were an integral part of the US-led cocktail golden age that started in the late 1800s. Chartreuse is made by French monks who standardized their recipe in 1764. That's hundreds of years of work spanning four countries that went into making this cocktail!

RD | 75

Petit Ermitage | *Belle*
From entrance to front desk, hallway to stairs, bar to loungy rooftop restaurant, this place is gorgeous. It's absolutely slathered with Moroccan design elements, resulting in a space that has a classic, luxurious, and exotic feel. The Belle cocktail is named after the hotel's signature suite and it tastes as classic and luxurious as the bespoke design looks and feels. It uses two time-tested spirits that have been around for centuries; Laird's Apple Brandy is made by a family who have been distilling apples on the US's East Coast since Colonial times and the recipe for Benedictine Liqueur is said to be 500 years old. Petit Ermitage is about as exclusive as it gets. If you find your way in, enjoy every second and every sip!

RD | 77

Stache | *Somebody to Love*
If you're looking for a reason to drink, this cocktail is a really good one because Somebody to Love is made with fresh green juice! Certainly, that means it's healthy for you. Right? It's at least good on the taste buds. Casamigos Tequila and Scrappy's Fire Tincture give it a nice kick. If you get to visit this fun bar, make sure to check out the walls in the bathroom stalls.

RD | 79

Trunks Bar | *Casamigos Mezcal Shot*
Trunks serves their Casamigos Mezcal with a slice of orange for a lovely pairing. This shot is the perfect thing to have whether you're spending your Sunday afternoon watching football or heading to the dance floor.

CITY CENTER

CC | 85

Conservatory (R.I.P.) | *Sex in LA*

I haven't been a fan of cocktails with candy in them since sometime in the aughts—until this one. Sex in LA changed everything! It isn't overly sweet like you might expect; in fact, there's plenty of tart in there providing balance. The lychee cotton candy they developed for it was a lovely touch. Sadly, the only place you can get one of these cocktails now is from your own kitchen, because this spot has since closed.

CC | 87

Delilah | *The JoJo*

The door closing behind you shuts out the heat (and the line of people waiting to get in). You enjoy the cool air against your face while you wait for your eyes to adjust to the low light. Once they do, you relax into one of the banana plant-shrouded velvet booths where the quiet but confident hum of a room full of beautiful people flirting with one another surrounds you. The JoJo, named for a late family dog, is like delicious, fruity air conditioning for the palate. Sipping this luscious libation while ensconced in Delilah's big band-era ambiance transports you to a glamorous Hollywood past.

CC | 89

Hamburger Mary's | *Bellini*

A little irreverence can be a good thing and Hamburger Mary's does it perfectly. Having a drink served to you in a leg shaped cup is very fitting here, especially if you're drinking out of it while watching one of their famous drag shows. It's EXTRA special if you're sipping a Hamburger Mary's Bellini during Drag Brunch, which can get so raucous that sometimes the performers take the show out onto the street outside!

CC | 91

Hugo's | *Bloody Mary | Michelada*

Late night last night? Walk-of-shame your way into this comfy, pajamas-welcomed, WeHo staple. The Bloody Mary mix they make in-house is yummy and might just help you perk up a bit (or maybe that perkiness is because of the Tito's Vodka they combine it with?). Pair that same mix with some Stone Buenaveza Salt & Lime Lager and you've got Hugo's delectable Michelada. Come in on a Friday evening to catch Drag Happy Hour!

CC | 93

La Bohème | *Maguey Picante*

This Dos Hombres Mezcal-based cocktail reflects the space where it was created. It's smoky, sophisticated, silky, and seductive but also dark, dangerous (beware the worms!), and damn delicious. The salt is a really intriguing touch (unless you're a vegetarian). To make it, actual worms are harvested from agave plants, dried, ground, and mixed with salt and spices.

CC | 95

Laurel Hardware | *L.A. Rosa*

From the street, Laurel Hardware looks like an old hardware store (because it was and they've kept the original façade). You walk in and rather than a hardware store, the space opens up to a beautiful bar and restaurant. They have a great cocktail menu and the L.A. Rosa is one of their stand-outs! It's a delicious combo of Calirosa Rosa Blanco Tequila (aged in red wine barrels), Los Angeles-made Liquid Alchemist syrups, a floral aperitivo, and SO much strawberry. It modernizes the idea and structure of an old-school Tiki cocktail offering the drinker a whole new class of tropical libations.

CC | 97

Norah | *Blackbird*

This Bombay Sapphire-based cocktail is a GREAT option for anyone who thinks they don't like gin. It's crisp, bright, and fruity and the gin masterfully underpins the other ingredients without taking over in the least. Sustainability shout-out to Norah's team for dehydrating the used ingredients from their Thai basil shrub to make its rimming salt, no waste here!

CC | 99

Phorage WeHo | *Pho-Mojito*

A clever play on a Mojito, Phorage's mixologist team created their Pho-Mojito by taking the typical white rum base and infusing it with the spices used in pho (Vietnamese noodle soup). They also add Thai basil (which comes on the side when you order pho) to the traditional mint garnish. This restaurant has done other interesting things too, like having another restaurant, a Detroit style pizzeria, nestled inside of it during covid (now moved to its permanent home in Canoga Park)! As a child of Detroit, I was so excited to see staples of the Great Lakes State like Faygo soda and beer from Bell's Brewery.

Written by Sarah L.M. Mengoni

CC | 101

Surly Goat | *Craft Beer*
Come to the Surly Goat to find a great beer selection! Despite there being lots of breweries in Southern California, Los Angeles just isn't much of a beer town. West Hollywood is lucky to have a place that carries and celebrates all kinds of craft beers on draft. The handles change regularly, so there's always something new and interesting.

CC | 103

Ysabel | *Ysabel Margarita*
This is about as well made a Margarita as you'll get. It omits the orange liqueur in favor of agave nectar, which is a style known as a Tommy's Margarita that was developed in California and has become popular across the country. Ysabel is doing it wonderfully, pairing it with a reposado tequila (Cazadores) and adding orange bitters.

SUNSET STRIP

SS | 109

Andaz West Hollywood | *Paradise City*
Tropics flirt with the desert and chic elements class up the kitsch in this cabana cocktail with a well-matched blend of Casamigos Reposado Tequila, coconut, pineapple, and cinnamon. It's served over crushed ice and is so fun and delicious that I dare you to drink it and not have a riotous good time.

SS | 111

BOA Steakhouse | *Bee Blossom*
This is a really nice variation of the classic Bee's Knees cocktail. The fresh marigold and tiny honey popsicle they use to garnish it play well with the Roku Gin base. All of the ingredients come together to taste like a pastoral summer day. The restaurant's vibe is perfect for this bright and airy steakhouse. With each sip you can practically hear happy bees buzzing and mellow cows mooing.

SS | 113

The Classic Cat | *Burlesque Fuse*
Walking through the velvet curtain into The Classic Cat takes you from the bright lights, noise, and hustle of The Sunset Strip into a sultry feast of pinks and golds, padded booths, feathers, and tantalizing artwork. The Burlesque Fuse drinks well amidst all that sensuousness. It's a sexified spritz, loaded with fresh berries and elevated by the addition of Neft Vodka and fancy bitters.

SS | 115

The DEN on Sunset | *Spicy Paloma*
Not only is the Paloma a West Hollywood favorite, it's also gaining popularity all over the country. Using serrano pepper-infused Cazadores Tequila is a nice addition to the classic. When Katie took me to try late-night drinks at The DEN, it was definitely a party at this neighborhood institution.

SS | 117

Lobby Bar (The West Hollywood EDITION) | *Lost in Tarzana*
A cool, crisp cocktail served in a cool, crisp space. Why are we Lost in Tarzana, a city across the hills in the San Fernando Valley? I'm not sure, but with this drink in hand, it doesn't even matter— it'd be fun to be lost just about anywhere. Del Maguey Vida is an excellent cocktail mezcal, and the Chareau Aloe provides a subtle minty flavor.
Bonus points if you can figure out where the light shining on the pool table originates.

SS | 119

Eveleigh | *Sibling Warfare*
As we walked into this bar, I was thinking that we really needed to put a cocktail in this book that didn't have tequila in it. West Hollywood LOVES tequila and mezcal, so the recipes were skewing in that direction. As it was my job to make sure we included more than just agave cocktails (agave is the plant tequila and mezcal are made from), I was looking for something different, like whiskey, for example. Then Katie and I sat at the bar and met Johnny. He presented us with his Sibling Warfare and it was delicious! Irresistible! A standout! So good, in fact, that it had to go in this book. So, what was it made with? BOTH tequila and mezcal, of course!

SS | 121

Harriet's | *Skyline*
Come for the view, stay for the Kuleana Rum Agricole cocktail! What's rum agricole, you ask? Well, most rum is made from the by-products of refining sugar (molasses). Agricole is made using fresh pressed cane juice (what sugar is made from), which ferments SUPER fast. It's dry, complex, grassy, and SO different from other styles of rum. These unique flavors make it beloved by craft bartenders and combine deliciously with the other ingredients in this drink.

SS | 123   **Hotel Ziggy |** *Witchy Woman*
This hotel is so rock 'n' roll! The Witchy Woman fits the space perfectly. With its fuchsia color and black salt rim it's beautiful and alluring but also feels a little dangerous. It tastes great and the vanilla notes from the Casamigos Reposado really pop.

SS | 125   **Hotel Ziggy |** *Jameson Orange Sticky Toffee Pudding*
Judging by this pudding, Katie Brightside isn't just an incredibly talented artist, she's also a great baker! She had the brilliant idea to develop this recipe just for the book. I helped by being her taster and eating as much of it as she'd put in front of me. It's perfectly moist and sweet with the nicest little hint of orange.
Huge shout out to the tasting team, Luis, Jamison, Todd, and Chance.

SS | 127   **Juniper Lounge (1 Hotel West Hollywood) |** *Eagle Rocked*
Stirred, spirits-forward cocktails are tough to find in this part of the world, as WeHo tends to prefer light and crushable drinks. But there's so much more out there! What would cocktail culture be without the sophisticated Manhattans and Old Fashioneds?! Juniper does well at filling this void. They use Calirosa Añejo Tequila as a base for this boozy, silky cocktail that perfectly balances bitter with sweet.

SS | 129   **Justin Queso's |** *JQ's Ranch Water*
A Ranch Water is the perfect cocktail for this Tex-Mex spot, as its origins seem to be from West Texas. The story goes that when ranch workers took a break, they would drink a little out of their bottle of Topo Chico, then squeeze some lime and pour some tequila into the bottle. Effing genius! This drink contains a high ratio of soda and lime to tequila, so it's very light, VERY crushable, and keto friendly! Justin Queso's puts their JQ's Ranch Water in a pint glass, uses blanco tequila, and adds a Tajin rim.
Bring your dog in for their Bone Appetit menu!

SS | 131   **Katana LA |** *Tropical Hibiscus*
The name, Tropical Hibiscus, says it all! This concoction is loaded with tropical flavors and is nice and tart from the hibiscus and lime. It's made with Dahlia Cristalino; cristalino is a tequila style that is aged in barrels, then filtered to remove the color while leaving the flavor from aging. The style has been around for a while and is finally starting to gain popularity in tequila-crazy West Hollywood.

SS | 133   **The London West Hollywood at Beverly Hills |** *Panoma 94*
Sometimes people don't want to drink alcohol. Whether it's for safety reasons (you're the designated driver-don't drink and drive!), health reasons, or ANY reason, choosing not to drink the hard stuff shouldn't make anyone feel excluded from social situations or left out of the pleasure of drinking cocktails. To accommodate those non-boozy drinkers, many bars are now offering alcohol-free drinks that are treated with the same creativity as their spirited brethren. The London offers a selection of well executed non-alcoholic mocktails. This Paloma variation is one of them and is a delight to drink. They use Seedlip 94 as the base spirit. Seedlip is doing a great job of using distillation (the process that's used to make hard liquor) to make spirits that *don't* contain any alcohol.

SS | 135   *Nikko Niigata*
The London's cocktail menu is loaded with fun ingredients. Japanese-produced Shibui Grain Select is a whisky with lots of tropical notes. This made it a great choice to mix with the flavors of fresh pineapple juice and Liquid Alchemist Passion Fruit Syrup. The combination results in a delightful concoction that highlights those island flavors, but is still light and citrusy.

SS | 137   **The Naughty Pig |** *Vodka Soda*
Every neighborhood needs a place like The Naughty Pig—a spot without pretension, where the drinks are strong, the music is loud (but not too loud to talk over), and the staff is friendly and FUN. This Kástra Elión soda is exactly what you want to drink at such a place. It doesn't skimp on the vodka and it goes down smooth and easy. Bartenders love bars like this. Stop by at the end of the night and you're likely to see somebody who made you a cocktail earlier in the evening. If you do, buy that hardworking M*f*er a drink!

Written by Sarah L.M. Mengoni

SS | 139

Bar Pendry (Pendry West Hollywood) | *Pomegranate Fizz*
Fresh pomegranate juice makes this cocktail exceptional. It blends perfectly with Absolut Elyx Vodka and orange curaçao. These, and the rest of the ingredients result in a cocktail that is tart, sweet, light, and flavorful. This delightful drink is being served in an equally delightful space that feels like old Hollywood, a contemporary art museum, and a sunset at the beach all rolled into one.

SS | 141

Rainbow Bar & Grill | *Jack & Coke*
What is more rock 'n' roll than a Jack & Coke at the iconic Rainbow Bar & Grill?! Sit at any of the red booths and be confident that the biggest of big-name rock stars from decades past sat there before you. Just imagine what happened on, and under those tables!

SS | 143

Rock & Reilly's | *Irish Mule*
This is the place to go if you want to visit an Irish bar in West Hollywood. With sports on the TV, '90s hits blaring loud enough to get you hyped, and a good selection of Irish Whiskey, it's a fun spot to sit at the bar and make new friends. Their Irish Mules (made with Tullamore D.E.W. Irish Whiskey and Fever-Tree Ginger Beer) are incredibly appropriate given the West Hollywood origin of the Moscow Mule that inspired their creation.

SS | 145

The Roxy Theatre | *Tina's Delight*
If you don't know what The Roxy is, you ain't rock 'n' roll. And Tina knows rock 'n' roll. She was the spirits buyer for this legendary rock club for ages. While in this powerful role she saw a space in the market for a non-gmo, organic, woman-owned vodka, so she went out and made one!

SS | 147

Skybar (Mondrian LA) | *The Red Headed Mule*
Simplicity wins in this version of a Moscow Mule made with fresh raspberries, Ketel One Vodka, and Q Mixers Ginger Beer. The bar's poolside location and its amazing city views have been attracting the most beautiful people in LA for years.

SS | 149

State Social House | *Cigar Pairing*
This spot reminds me of the old-school bars that I loved to hang out at during my time in Chicago. Regulars sipping whiskey, local beers on tap, and a bartender who seems as much a character as a real person make State Social House a staple. And, it's the only cigar bar in West Hollywood. If you're already a cigar aficionado, we bow to your prowess. But in case you, like us, are novices in the cigar world, we recommend the pairing of an Ashton Cigar, Tortuga Isabella White Ale, and The Macallan 12 to get you started. You may want to bring your own lighter as only matches are provided (apparently the bar lighters tend to walk off).
Thanks to owner Robert and local Derrick for helping us newbies out!

SS | 151

Sunset Marquis | *Honeydew Me*
Sotol is made primarily in the Mexican region of the Chihuahuan Desert. It's distilled from the Dasylirion plant, a distant relative of agave. The flavor can vary but it tends to be grassy and earthy. It is used beautifully in this cocktail, which blends the Quechōl Sotol with melon and herbs to create a drink that is elegant, light, and absolutely delicious.

SS | 153

Tesse Restaurant | *Pea Diddy*
This must-try is both a cocktail nerd's dream and a casual drinker's delight! It tastes like a glass full of an afternoon spent in a summer garden. I really can't recommend it highly enough. And it's versatile! When peas aren't in season they turn the Pea Diddy into the Bad Bunny, also made with Kástra Elión Vodka, aquavit, and anisette but combined with carrot, ginger, and bird's eye chili.
Are you a hungry carnivore with a thirst for adventurous drinking? Order the Bucatini and add a Madeira Bone Luge.

SS | 155

Tower Bar (Sunset Tower Hotel) | *Tower Smash*
This art deco hotel is the epitome of class inside and out. Visiting the Tower Bar feels like you're sliding onto a stool during the Golden Age of Hollywood. The refreshing tequila-based Tower Smash is in a class of its own and it perfectly complements the bar's wood-paneled sophistication.

Warrior Bar (R.I.P.) | *Morning Glory*
Suntory Toki is light as far as whisky goes, which lets the flavor of the Frosted Flakes it's infused with come through. The combo results in an Old Fashioned variation that's more delicate than one would expect—and super fun. This hidden gem of a bar was eclectic and sexy. Sadly the bar has closed since we were there doing our research, though the space is available for events.

LIFE HACK
Earthbar | *Liver Cleanse*
Out late last night? Feeling a little groggy? This is the perfect drink to reset and invigorate your body and mind. The Liver Cleanse, made with fresh fruits, beets, ginger, and aloe perfectly balances sweet, spicy, and tangy to help you become your best and brightest self. Now get out there and get on with your plans for the new day!

Next Health West Hollywood
Next Health suggests that you do the following three therapies in the order they are listed here, which they referred to as the "One-Stop-Shop," prior to heading out for a night at the bars in this book. Before taking any of these therapies, please check in with your medical provider to make sure these treatments are right for you given whatever health conditions and/or needs you currently have. We're not medical experts.

Infrared LED Sauna Therapy
You lie down in pod-like beds for your infrared sauna treatment. I swear it's as hot as an August day visit to the core of the sun in that pod and in retrospect I wouldn't have eaten anything heavy before putting my tummy in that kind of heat. Your head sticks out of the bed which is helpful in keeping the heat bearable. I came out feeling jittery and weak, like after a good run. And just like after a good run, a few minutes and some cold water later, I felt pretty great. I was ready for a night of cocktail tasting with Katie!

Hangover IV Drip
Before the needle goes into your arm, the staff here start making you feel cozy and comfortable. The seats are big and cushy, and you get a pillow to hold on to. They even have some baller massage chairs you can sit in. During IV drips you often get a taste in your mouth from what's being pumped in; with this one I got some of that vitamin B taste but not much. By the time it was done the headache I walked in with had disappeared. A half an hour after we finished I noticed that Katie's eyes, which had been puffy and tired from the night before, were back to bright and sparkly.

Cryotherapy
I hate the cold. Like REALLY hate the cold. Getting into a cryotherapy chamber, with a temperature less than -150˚, sounded like about the worst idea ever. But in the name of research for this book, I had to do it. So, I bucked up, stripped down, put on the towel, socks and gloves they gave me (they also have masks and hats), and stepped into the chamber. And you know what, it wasn't bad! They give you headphones to wear while you're inside, so I picked a song to sing-along to for the three minute thirty second duration. With the help of Alexander Hamilton and the entertaining faces Katie was making (we were in there together) time flew. I actually felt great when I got out! Totally energized.

BUILD YOUR OWN
Build Your Own THC Experience
The practice of sitting and rolling a joint or packing a bowl, then passing it amongst friends is one that is filled with little rituals that heighten the experience. Ingestible marijuana by nature isn't ritualistic—you just put it in your mouth. What we've tried to do with this Build Your Own is to create an experience that carries that ritualized aspect and can be enjoyed in a group.

Written by Sarah L.M. Mengoni

Afterword

Here we are readers; friends, at the end of our mutual journeys. I hope you've enjoyed your trip through the cocktails and history of West Hollywood. I have certainly enjoyed mine; though to be honest, it was a much harder and longer trip than I thought it would be.

At the time of my fateful introduction to Miss Katie Brightside, I was living in North Hollywood, CA, and working just across the hills in West Hollywood. I'd spent years studying and working with alcohol and behind bars. Those years had led me to the role of Lead Bartender at the La Peer Hotel. There, Katie and I were introduced and a couple weeks later we met to discuss her project. I dragged along a bag full of my favorite cocktail books. We spent a great night in WeHo, bar hopping, poring over the books, and getting to know each other. We talked about her idea for *Once Upon a Cocktail*, started evolving the concept, and brainstormed other fun ideas like a cocktail competition. By the time Katie and I parted ways it was a done deal; I was in. After two decades of reading cocktail books, I was incredibly excited to be part of creating one.

We spent the next eight months traipsing around the city, surrounded by bright lights, lots of people, and the particular high energy that this sliver of the world carries. I was turned into a tourist in my own town. I didn't really understand how walkable West Hollywood was before our adventures. I'd been yearning for this the entire time I'd lived in Los Angeles, chained to my car. Katie doesn't even have a car! So, we rode our sneakers to just about every bar in the city (Katie wore out so many pairs working on this book). Some visits were short, walking in and walking right back out. Others were long, with multiple cocktail tastings and dinner. We were choosing places as much as we were choosing cocktails, trying to put ourselves in our reader's walking shoes, to figure out what places would best represent West Hollywood.

We experienced fine dining, old Hollywood haunts, clubs, neighborhood bars, and dives. I was so enchanted and enthralled by the architecture, billboards, people, dogs, and cats surrounding us that Katie always had quite a job of herding me down the street and keeping me from wandering into traffic. I spent an entire afternoon completely distracted by a kitten that Katie dubbed "One-Eyed Willie." a representative from the Springboard Hospitality Group was generously spending his time taking us to visit the bars in the hotels that he oversaw. He had Willie and another tiny kitten with him because they didn't have a mom anymore. They were so young they had to be hand-fed. Willie was a black and white tuxedo kitty with—you guessed it—one eye. That tiny handful of snuggly fluff had me wrapped around his adorable paw. I cuddled Willie against my chest as we drove to and toured the four Springboard hotels in WeHo. This meant I took next to zero notes, which did create more work later. It was worth it! Incidentally, Katie tried to cuddle Willy's sibling, but gave up when it relieved itself on her.

While we were traipsing around, playing with all the kittens and beverages West Hollywood had to offer, I was curating the cocktails for the book. Obviously, it was important to have drinks that were delicious. But they also needed to represent the place they were served and to fit within the overall harmony of the book. It would have been very easy to have a book that was filled with sixty Margarita variations (WeHo loves its tequila!) but that wasn't the book that we wanted. We were after a book that had different styles of cocktails, varied flavors, and many types of spirits represented. It needed to be balanced, like a good drink menu is balanced, with something for everyone. It turned out though that we were curating more than just cocktails, we were curating places as well.

Some of those places are incredible craft cocktail bars on par with the best bars I've visited across the United States and Europe. If you're a beer drinker we've led you to the Surly Goat. Cigar smoker? State Social House. We've got music venues, dance clubs, celebrity hangouts, and on and on. We achieved the balance we knew we were looking for with the drinks themselves, but also, and somewhat unexpectedly, with the bars as well. Looking at them now, all together, I sincerely believe that the drinks and the *places to drink* in this book are an excellent representation of the nature of drinking in West Hollywood: it's remarkable in both its options and quality.

Written by Sarah L.M. Mengoni

That time of discovery was a magical time in the process of the book, and I was honestly sad when it came to an end. But we still had so much work to do, even more than we realized.

The next step was recipe testing. The various bars had given us the recipes for their cocktails. Now we needed to make sure that, when followed, they came out tasting the way they were supposed to and that they were actually possible to make at home. This testing required a ton of preparation. We spent a couple days planning and building spreadsheets together. We needed to be sure we were getting every single ingredient that was in all the drinks. Katie walked from bar to bar collecting samples of spirits. We both went grocery shopping. I pulled bottles from my home bar, visited my local specialty liquor store, and bought some tools I thought we might need.

We scheduled three days for the actual testing. We hired my friend RJ Chesney, who I'd worked with previously, to come and be my assistant those three days. We set up lights and cameras around my home bar so Katie could record the process while I made drinks. We even invited guests to come sit at the bar! It was quite an honor to have drink masters like Maxwell Reis and Heidi Wittekind pay a visit to my little apartment. Those days were FUN! They were also hard work and long—lasting 14 hours each. They were critical though. During the testing we found recipes where clarification was needed, and others with prep that was just too hard to make. It would have been insurmountable without the skills of RJ, who basically lived in my small galley kitchen those three days, knocking out prep recipe after prep recipe after prep recipe.

Once the recipe testing wrapped, it was time for me to start writing. Recipe pages were first. No sweat, I thought; each one couldn't possibly take more than 15 minutes. HAH! I was so wrong. I ended up spending several hours on every single one. It was so much more complicated than I anticipated. I thought wording the recipes so that they were easy to understand would be the hardest part. Nah. Keeping the wording consistent from page to page, changing measurements from weight to volume so they could be measured without a scale, checking juiced fruit and veggie output so I knew how much to tell people to prepare—it was all so much more than I thought it would be. What I thought I would have finished by the end of September, took me until January to complete.

After the recipes, I wrote a glossary to cover tools, terms, techniques and glassware as well as the cocktail Tasting Notes. Those things all had their hiccups as well, but nothing too crazy. So here we are, well over a year since Katie brought me on to this incredible project. My life has changed dramatically over the time I've been contributing my efforts to this book. A few weeks after recipe testing finished, my hubby and I packed my bar (and other important possessions) into a van and started a year's sojourn traveling the States. Working in a tiny space and dealing with the complications that come with living on the road only helped to slow down my progress on *Once Upon a Cocktail*. But here I am now, living a dream life, writing the last few sentences of a dream project.

So, we've all come to the end of this journey. But it's not really over for any of us. I hope that you enjoy referring to these recipes and their stories over and over again. And I'll continue to explore the rest of the country with the same enthusiasm that Katie and I explored West Hollywood. Who knows, maybe there's another *Once Upon a Cocktail* destination waiting to be discovered...

I will be eternally grateful to Katie Brightside for allowing me to be part of such a cool project, to the visionary Nick Rimedio for putting Katie and I together, to my dad Rod and my son Ricky (because without the two of you, there is no me), and to my beloved and supportive hubs, Mark, who's been very patient through all the hours I've spent ignoring him in favor of working.

Conclusion

How to conclude a cocktail book? DRINK! Since I've thrown out traditional rules on how to create a book, why should the conclusion be any different. The beginning of the book is in my voice and Sarah with her cocktail curating expertise, took over after the recipes.

It was suggested we have a Q+A-style-Conclusion where we both answer the same questions. Like the beginning and middle coming together at the end. So here we go—make sure you have something to sip in hand.

What was this book about?
K: In summary this book is about friendships and uniting people: the talented individuals that make up the city's bars, restaurants, hotels, sponsors, and brand partners. The whole city interacted, fueling the project, which allowed the book to become larger than life, its own entity, and a true representation of a neighborhood.

S: I think Katie and I feel similarly about this. It's so much more than a collection of recipes. It's a book about community and the bars and restaurants that help set the tone for areas of the city. At its heart are the personalities that lead those venues, the brand representatives that support them, and the people who frequent them. The coming together of all those individuals is the true soul of this book.

What was this book personally about for you?
K: It is The American Dream fulfilled—an idea that was watered and nurtured that grew to be fruitful. I have been humbled by the whole process. To have participated in creating a vehicle that connect people in LA fills me with tearful gratitude for the experience.

S: Fulfilling dreams and creating opportunities. I've been a huge fan and collector of cocktail books for years and have always had fantasies of creating my own. I was just waiting for an original concept to come to me. Katie brought that novel idea! It seems that every new thing I do opens unanticipated opportunities; I expect it will be the same with *Once Upon a Cocktail*. I'm very excited to discover what those will be!

Is there anything you would do again or differently?
K: I wouldn't change or redo a thing on this one. I believe things happen for a reason and this book concluded in its own divine time, the way the Universe intended. However, I would definitely approach a new book differently, now knowing the steps that were created in this project. I'd create a process, plan, and enlist additional help.

S: I would apply the same standards again: tasting everything, experiencing every location, testing recipes, and rejecting things when necessary. This all ensures a level of quality that the reader deserves. As far as doing things differently, there are many technical aspects of my work that could have been completed more efficiently. As an example, when the amazing RJ was prepping for recipe checks, I would have had him record volume measurements of everything he juiced and everything he measured by weight. That would have saved me multiple hours of work and headaches while I was writing the recipes.

What was the point of no return for you? When were you either hooked or you had invested too much?
K: Walking 30 miles in two days in 35 °C heat (96 °F) with small containers of booze from the bars for recipe check was a trial. Why not a car? Driving is always subjective to congestion and parking—and I don't have one. West Hollywood is easy to navigate on foot. I know how long it will take, down to the minute, to get to a destination. Those two days were hard going. Who thought I needed to do a recipe check? Doh! By this point, both Sarah and I were hard and fast committed. It was the point of no return and we did everything in our power to make sure this book was the best and as accurate as we could make it.

S: Let's be real, I was hooked after the first night that Katie and I spent discussing her idea for the book.

Was there a low point?
K: When I had to go all black-ops and remove myself from human existence to focus and complete the book. I deleted myself from social media and stopped returning messages. I may have even *not* remembered to shower for days! It's the creative process that people do when they need to hyperfocus—writing an album, book, or creating a dream. In this space there is no 9-5; it will be done when it's done! It's a contradiction, as a version of me cherishes this period, but day after day, no end in sight, can be hard to truck on. If you're a friend and haven't experienced this level of drive, it's hard to understand why "fun Katie" is not available right now.

Written by Katie Brightside & Sarah L.M. Mengoni

S: A few weeks prior to Katie and I being introduced I had returned to my job after months being laid up due to the flare-up of a spinal injury. Continually having to take time from the project to rest when my body told me to was anticipated, but very frustrating. In addition to dealing with that injury, just after recipe checks and before beginning the writing for *Once Upon a Cocktail*, I started a year-long trip around the country in a van. This wonderful once-in-a-lifetime change in lifestyle came with issues around connectivity to the internet and power for my laptop. Both these things contributed to my anxiety around not being able to get work done when I needed to. The most surprising thing; however, was my difficulty in adjusting to the loss of regular paychecks. Watching my savings dwindle and not knowing when or where the next check was coming from spun me out; I wasted a lot of time chasing small change. With some helpful pep talks from friends (including Katie herself), I was able to let go of my fear and embrace the reality that I had planned for this and would be fine. In the words of Hunter S. Thompson, "Full speed ahead and damn the cost, it will all come out in the wash."

What was the high point?

K: I have numerous high points, but seeing Sarah's face light up, surprised by a venue or finding a drink that inspired her neural pathways into fireworks was my hands-down favorite. Watching Sarah's process was insightful. I learnt so much from her; Sarah's a great teacher, peer, and comrade. FOR LIFE! mahaha

S: Like Katie, I had so many highs during this process. But the best thing was getting to know Katie herself. What a special thing to find, an understanding and kind collaborator, an inspiring mentor, and a great friend all in the same beautiful person.

What was a funny moment?

K: The teasing and playful misdirection to suggest cute, adorable fluffy things in sight, so when Sarah turns to look, I could swig any of the ten cocktails in front of her. Confused, she'd return focus to the task in hand realizing I had swindled her, abusing her weakness for neon, sparkly, or furry—to be honest it could be anything tangible. Last week, when I called her in Vangoni, she paused the conversation to look at a alligator in a swamp and an incredible looking well-engineered bridge.

S: Katie has a wonderful English accent that basically makes everything sound charming. This includes her *Bloody Brilliant British* phrasing... and her repeated mis-pronunciation of tricky words like reposado.

Did anything surprise you?

K: That I'd be writing this conclusion! Am I really here? Is this a dream? The book ended up being four times the size as we'd originally intended. To be here is a long-awaited surprise!

S: EVERYTHING TOOK FOUR TIMES LONGER THAN I THOUGHT IT WOULD.

What key thing did you learn?

K: That a project may start with one intention that may twist and turn to become something more, something that you would never dream of. *Once Upon a Cocktail* became its own entity, with its own story to teach and I was privileged to be on the carpet ride, holding onto the corner, flying into the unknown.

S: Investing in bold dreams means going all in, not letting worries about time and money distract you.

What's next for the book?

K: Covering all the towns in all the world; so the *Once Upon a Cocktail* team might soon be walking into yours!

S: I hope for the success of this book so we can create more in other cities.

What's next for the brand?

K: Receiving the *Once Upon a Cocktail* trademark I registered for, a coffee table book, and a mixology competition. For the latter, I want to bring back the no-man's-land of West Hollywood, The Sunset Strip law, that no rules are the rules. I'd like a contest where gambling and cheating are encouraged. TBC...

S: Katie has such vision, I'm honored to be here to help her come up with ideas and fulfill her always audacious goals.

What's next for you personally?

K: A shower!

S: Another dream project! I'll be making videos and writing articles about the fascinating boozy history and culture I discovered as I traveled. You can find them at historically-drinking.com

Cocktail Terms & Techniques

Big Ice Cube
A 2" ice cube. Can be made in special large molds, or purchased from some specialty spirits stores. The bigger cube melts slower than smaller ice, keeping your drink cold without watering it down.

Burnt Peel
To burn a peel, take a lighter or match and move it along the rind of your peel until the citrus oils become aromatic, then express the burnt oils onto your cocktail.

Citrus Wedges
Typically, you'll be cutting your citrus into eight total wedges. To do this, cut your citrus fruit in half from end to end. In each half cut a slit from side to side through the pulp without cutting into the rind (this slit will allow the finished wedge to sit on the rim of your glass). Turn the fruit over and cut each half into four pieces, again end to end. This will yield you your eight pieces.

Citrus Wheels
This works best with firm fruit. Cut and discard the pith ends from your citrus fruit. Slice perpendicular to the ends to create thin wheel shapes. Cut a small slit through the rind so that the citrus wheel can perch on the rim of your glass.

Chilled Glassware
It may seem obvious, but a cold cocktail should be very cold. If you pour your perfectly chilled cocktail into a room temperature glass, it will start warming the cocktail before it's even touched your lips. To chill a glass, you can either put the glass in a freezer for a few minutes or let ice water sit in it while you prepare the cocktail(s). Discard the ice water before pouring the cocktail into the glass.

Cocktail Cherry
Not to be confused with the neon red maraschino cherries that are often used in Shirley Temples, and whose stems you probably learned to tie with your tongue, if you ever worked in a bar that carried the monstrosities. Nope. The cherries you want have a natural, beautiful deep maroon color. They're often sour cherries that have been preserved in sugar syrup.

Double Strain
This technique combines two strainers to remove any small solid bits (herbs, fruits, egg, and even ice) out of your liquid before it lands in your glass. Pour through a Hawthorne Strainer directly into a fine mesh strainer that's positioned over your glass.

Dry Shake
Shaking without ice.

Dump
Pour the cocktail directly into the glass from the container it was made in, no straining needed.

Express
Squeezing a citrus peel (see "peel") from the sides to release the oils from the skin into your cocktail and/or glass.

Fine Strain
Pouring through a fine mesh strainer to remove small particles.

Float
Creating a layer of a liquid on top of your cocktail. To do this, place the tip of a bar spoon, bowl side down (facing the drink), against the surface of your cocktail where it meets the side of your glass. Slowly, and gently, pour the liquid to be floated over the back of your spoon.

Written by Sarah L.M. Mengoni

A List of Terms and Techniques
That are Useful to Know When
Making the Cocktails in This Book

Hard Shake/Light Shake

Imagine your normal cocktail shaker shake. Now imagine shaking it harder or lighter, when that's what the recipe calls for. A hard shake will add extra water and aeration to a cocktail that needs it; a light shake uses less agitation and adds less water to more delicate cocktails.

Heated Glassware

Same idea as glassware chilling, but for when you're serving a hot cocktail. Fill the glass with hot water and let it sit while you prepare the cocktail(s).

Ice (see also Rocks and Big Cube)

Ice is used to add water (from melting during shaking and stirring), provide aeration (during shaking), and of course to chill. Ice that is bigger and more solid melts slower, cooling thoroughly and adding less water. Ice that is smaller and more crumbly melts quickly, cools less and adds a greater amount of water. Consider the ice you choose to be one of the most important ingredients for your cocktails; and like any other ingredient, you want it to be both high quality and fit the drink's needs.

Neat

A drink served without ice. Usually used in reference to a spirit and not a cocktail but can be applied to cocktails served in bucket style glasses with no ice.

Peel

The swath of skin that a "Y peeler" (see Tools, page 188) removes from a piece of citrus fruit.

Pith

The white part of citrus that's between the peel and the fruit. Pith is bitter and is best avoided when peeling your fruit.

Rimmed

Place the rim of your glass into or against a liquid substance (rubbing the flesh of a lime or orange around the rim works great) before dipping it into a powdery or granular substance, such as rimming a glass with salt for a Margarita. Consider rimming only half the glass; this enables the drinker to modulate the amount they want or to take the option to sip without the rim.

Roll

A mixing technique used instead of shaking or stirring. You pour the cocktail from one tin (or glass) to another, rolling it back and forth. The pouring action aerates the cocktail without adding as much water from the ice as shaking does.

Sous Vide

This technique uses an "immersion circulator" (see Tools, page 187) to cook and thoroughly infuse items (with herbs, spices, etc.) by placing them in a vacuumed sealed plastic bag (or similar technique that removes all the air) and immersing that bag in a heated water bath at a consistently controlled low temperature for a specified amount of time. This technique is commonly used in professional bar kitchens to infuse spirits.

If you don't have an immersion circulator at home, you can use a crockpot, a laser thermometer, and a lot of patience and time to sous vide. Use the thermometer to determine when the water in the pot is the right temperature, then submerge the sous vide bag in the water. For the duration of time that your item(s) need to slow cook, you'll need to stand by the pot, point your thermometer at it, and lift and/or close the lid as needed to maintain a steady temperature.

Rocks
Ice.

Skewer(ed)
A pointy object that pokes through garnishes to hold them in place and/or make them easier to retrieve from the glass. A toothpick, for example, could be used to skewer cocktail cherries.

Twist
Often used interchangeably with "peel." A twist is actually a skinny and long piece of peel that is removed from the fruit using a "channel knife" (see Tools, page 187) and is sometimes called a pigtail.

Up
A drink that is shaken or stirred and served in a stemmed glass without ice.

Water Displacement
An alternative technique to vacuum sealing that's used to force air out of a plastic bag prior to cooking sous vide by partially immersing the open bag under the water, until the water has pushed (displaced) all of the air out, at which point you can seal the bag.

Whisk(e)y Spelling
Whiskey can be spelled with or without the "e." American and Irish producers generally use it, Canadian, Scottish, and Japanese producers usually don't.

Worm Salt (Sal de Gusano)
Loaded with umami, smoky, spicy, and salty flavors, the most titillating ingredient in this salt is worm larvae. The worms are harvested from agave plants in the mezcal producing regions of Mexico that would turn into moths, if they were left to munch on those precious agaves. After harvesting, they're dried, ground, and mixed with salt and spices to produce delicious worm salt.

Cocktail Tools

A list of implements to assist in creating the recipes from this book.

Having the right tools makes any job easier; the very pleasant job of constructing cocktails is no different. Here is a list of what you need to make every drink in this book like a real pro-bartender. Where can you find professional-quality bar tools? Barfly is a great resource, their Essential Deluxe Mixing Cocktail Kit is a good starting point (scan the QR code on page 188 for a direct link to purchase). You can also get most of the individual tools listed here from the Barfly® Mixology Gear Amazon site. And if you really want to immerse yourself in mixology, Barfly's 19-Piece Cocktail Set includes even more of the items listed here.

The first five items on this list, the most important for your home bar, are included in the Barfly Essential Deluxe Mixing Cocktail Kit.

Mixing Tin Set
A small tin that fits inside of a larger tin. Barfly makes good sets that have capped bottoms (an extra piece of metal affixed to each tin). This increases their durability, and the added weight makes them easier to shake.

Jigger
This measuring implement is very important when making cocktails. Would you bake a cake without measuring your ingredients? No! Making a great cocktail is similar in that its success heavily relies on balancing the ingredients. It's science!

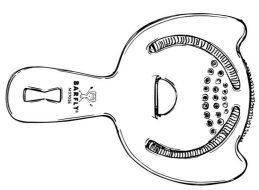

Hawthorne Strainer
The most ubiquitous strainer in cocktail bars, the spring clings to the inside of your tin while you're pouring.

Bar Spoon
This is used both for stirring cocktails and for measurement.

Mixing Glass
Used for stirred drinks. Stirring cocktails gives them an entirely different texture. Try stirring your Margarita instead of shaking it and you'll see what I mean.

Written by Sarah L.M. Mengoni

Atomizer
This very small bottle has a spray nozzle that separates the liquid coming out of it into a fine mist. This is different from a more typical spray nozzle that releases much bigger droplets. We want a fine mist, tiny droplets that will hover over the top of our cocktails and around the glass like a perfume.

Blender
Pulverizes your ingredients.

Channel Knife
This handheld tool has a v-shaped metal piece sticking out of it. When the v is dug along the skin of a citrus fruit it creates a long and skinny piece of peel that is used as a garnish.

Cheesecloth
Used to strain the very small particles out of a liquid that are even too small for a fine strainer. If you don't have cheesecloth, you can use a coffee filter.

Dehydrator
Uses low temperatures over many hours to remove the moisture from whatever foodstuffs you've put in it. If you don't have a dehydrator, you can use your oven on the lowest or "warm" setting.

Gram Scale
These are used to measure weight instead of volume, and are standard in professional kitchens. They are also useful in measuring very small quantities. Where possible, the recipes in this book use volume measurements for the ease of the reader.

Fine Strainer
Sometimes referred to as a tea strainer. It's important to use this fine mesh strainer after you've muddled something or shaken herbs into your cocktail. Otherwise, you and your guests will end up with bits of food stuck in between your teeth.

Hand Juicer
It can't be emphasized enough how important fresh juice is to making delicious cocktails, especially when it comes to lemon and lime juice! Try to juice right before you make your cocktail(s), or at least no more than 24 hours beforehand.

Immersion Circulator
This machine cooks items sous vide-style, which is when you seal items in a plastic bag after removing all the air and then slow cook it by immersing the bag in a water bath kept at one consistent low temperature.

Juicer
Extracts juice from your ingredients, separating it from the pulp. If you don't have a juicer, you can use a blender instead but you'll need to do some extra fine-straining afterwards. Note: Blender extraction does not yield as much juice as a juicer.

Large Cube Silicone Ice Tray
Use this to freeze big 2" x 2" ice cubes. Large cubes melt slower, so they cool your drink without watering it down as much as smaller cubes do.

Lemon Grater/Lemon Zester

These two hand-held tools serve similar functions. The grater is used to scrape the oil-filled peel into small bits. The zester (illustrated above) removes thin strings of shredded peel.

Lewis Bag and Mallet

These are used for crushing ice. Put your cubes in the bag and pound away your frustrations until there are no big chunks left.

Muddler

Used to extract the essence from things by lightly mashing them in the mixing tin. This works great, especially with fruit and veggies. Instead of muddling, herbs can be shaken with ice, which does a good job of bringing out the herb's aromatics without extracting unwanted bitterness.

Smoke Top

This is used to place a layer of smoke on top of your cocktail.

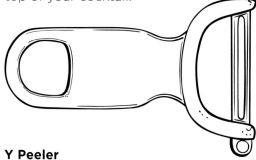

Y Peeler

Used to remove swathes of peel from citrus fruit.

>> "It is not the tools we use that make us good,

but rather how we employ them.

Upon failure, it is easier to blame the tools used rather than how they were employed."

- Traditional Proverb

>> **"Give us the tools, and we will finish the job."**

- Winston Churchill

Glassware

There's a lot of glassware out there! This list covers what is used for the recipes in this book. Often, the glassware a cocktail is served in has a purpose. Changing the glassware can change the perception, quality, and overall enjoyment of your drink. That said, if you don't have the glassware that's called for, use whatever is closest. You'll still be making a great cocktail!

Bucket Glasses
Rocks Glass, Old Fashioned: These short and squat glasses are used for spirits served "neat" or "on the rocks" (see Cocktail Terms & Techniques, page 183), as well as many other types of cocktails, especially those made without any type of carbonated sodas.

Copper Mug
This drink vessel was popularized by the Moscow Mule's rise to fame. And where was the Moscow Mule invented? Find out on page SS | 143!

Plastic Party Cup
Often used in movies during frat party and beer pong scenes.

Shot Glass
Come on now, we all know what this is; don't we?

Snifter
This glass has a big bowl and a narrow mouth and is classically used to serve brandy in. The shape of the bowl allows you to wrap your hands around it, which slightly warms the glass, and the spirits inside, causing more aroma to be released. The narrow opening funnels those aromas toward your nose. The recipe in this book calling for a small snifter (RD | 71) is a hot drink, which you can substitute a small mug for if needed (or a large mug, depending on how boozy you're feeling!).

Tall Glasses
Collins, Highball, Footed Highball: Tall, straight sided, and typically holds more volume than bucket glasses. These are mostly for cocktails that contain soda.

Up Glasses
Nick and Nora: The smallest of the up glasses, they are mostly used for drinks that are all booze, no non-alcoholic ingredients.

Coupe: A very versatile glass; its sides are curved and narrows at the rim. This both concentrates the aromas toward your nose and helps prevent you from sloshing the drink all over the place.

Martini: We all know this one, don't we, with its ubiquitous v-shaped glass? In the '90s, basically everything was served in this stylized up glass.

Vacation Glasses
Drinking out of these glasses makes you feel like you've been transported to a beach, the tropics, or somewhere hot and sultry. Crushed ice and exotic flavors are often used in the cocktails filling these glasses.

Hurricane Glass: Shaped like a curvaceous woman, the namesake of this glass is the famous tropical rum cocktail, the Hurricane.

Tropical Glass: Also known as a Tiki glass. Because of it's culturally appropriated history, many people in the bar community are moving away from the word Tiki and your authors couldn't agree more. Hence, our use and offering of tropical as a substitution.

Written by Sarah L.M. Mengoni

Source List

With a drink in hand and the *Once Upon a Cocktail book* spread open on our *Source List*, we wondered if anyone was ever going to hand type the long-arse URLs to search the original source material? After all, this is predominantly a cocktail recipe book.

I thought if you, dear reader, were a keen history buff and wanted to deep dive into more information on the Timeline, Nuggets, and Tasting Notes featured in this book you could check out the drop down *Source List* on the onceuponacocktailweho.com website, with hyperlinks for ease.

A HUGE thank you is due to Jon Ponder from the *West Hollywood History Center*, for all his research on the city's bars, restaurants, and hotels. For more information on the History Center, check out westhollywoodhistory.org

⟫⟫ **To deep dive, follow the white rabbit!**

Sarah L.M. Mengoni

A veteran barkeep, Sarah L.M. Mengoni cut her teeth working in Michigan beer dives and shot joints (before the law even allowed her to enjoy them), then moved to Chicago where she discovered and embraced the World of the Cocktail. Her enthusiasm for cocktail culture and gift for crafting unique recipes has earned her industry recognition, such as 50 Women to Watch in Hotel F&B magazine, as well as countless features in publications such as Imbibe, Food and Wine, Vogue, Forbes, GQ, and Time Out LA, to name a few.

Sarah is a graduate of the distinguished BAR 5-DAY program in New York City, which stands as one of the industry's top mixology certifications.

Currently, Sarah spends time between living in LA and traveling the US with her husband in a van named "Vangoni." Along the way, she's working as a bar consultant, spirits and cocktail educator, and is exploring the diverse and fascinating drinking cultures the country has to offer.

You can also find Sarah working on her passion project, *Historically Drinking*, on her website and YouTube, where she posts short, information-packed episodes on what, when, where, and how people have engaged with alcohol throughout history.

historically-drinking.com

Katie Brightside

Welcome to the Brightside, a creative agency, is the brainchild of international illustrator, artist, and designer Katie Brightside. The company is impassioned with a melting pot of creatives from vast spectrums of the arts and delivers unique design and artistic projects. The firm also houses *The Digs Collection*, a homeware company highlighting illustrated mural scale artwork, wallpaper, and handmade kimonos.

Brightside has secured several public art installations and personally received a WeHo Artist Grant, was an honoree of the Phyllis Morris Women in Leadership Award for Design and Entrepreneurship, and the John Chase accolade for Innovation of Art and Design at West Hollywood's Creative Business Awards.

Today, Brightside defies creative boundaries as the imagineer of *Once Upon a Cocktail – West Hollywood*, a recipe book featuring 54 most cherished venues across the city.

Graduating with a BA in fashion at Kingston University, UK, 2001, Brightside moved to Treviso, Italy, where she worked as a designer at United Colours of Benetton. In 2002 she relocated to Sydney, Australia. In 2012, the aMBUSH Gallery hosted her first of many solo art exhibitions. This successful exhibition inspired a thirst for further education, a MA Fine Art from Central Saint Martin (CSM), London. After graduation Brightside sought advice from a White Witch, asking where she would live happily-ever-after. A week later Katie fulfilled that prophecy by moving to West Hollywood.

welcometothebrightside.com

The End

"Is this the end?"

"Of course not. It's only the beginning."

Grease, 1978.

Do you think your city can match the story of West Hollywood?

Please send us your city suggestions.

>> # We need a drink!

drink@onceuponacocktail.world

SPEAKEASY

Once upon a Cocktail

GLADIATOR

10